LECTIONARY WORSHIP AIDS

Series III, Cycle B

BY B. DAVID HOSTETTER

CSS Publishing Co., Inc.
Lima, Ohio

LECTIONARY WORSHIP AIDS, SERIES III, CYCLE B

Copyright © 1993 by
The CSS Publishing Company, Inc.
Lima, Ohio

You may copy the material in this publication if you are the original purchaser, for use as it was intended (worship material for worship use; educational material for classroom use; dramatic material for staging and production). No additional permission is required from the publisher for such copying by the original purchaser only. Inquiries should be addressed to: The CSS Publishing Company, Inc., 628 South Main Street, Lima, Ohio 45804.

Library of Congress Cataloging-in-Publication Data
(Revised for volume 2)

Hostetter, B. David, 1926-
   Lectionary worship aids.

   Cycle A — Cycle B
   1. Worship programs.   I. Common lectionary (1992)
BV198.H66   1992   264'.34   92-29803
ISBN 1-55673-3556-1   (v. 1)
ISBN 1-55673-3622-3   (v. 2)

Scripture quotations are from the *New Revised Standard Version of the Bible*, copyright 1989 by the Division of Christian Education of the National Council of the Churches of Christ in the USA. Used by permission.

9347 / ISBN 1-55673-622-3   PRINTED IN U.S.A.

Dedicated to the memory of my parents
The Reverend Benjamin Hess Hostetter and
Martha Elizabeth Taylor Hostetter,
both of whom taught me to pray
and used no prayer book except
the Holy Bible

TABLE OF CONTENTS

An Order of Worship 7

Advent
    First Sunday In Advent 9
    Second Sunday In Advent 11
    Third Sunday In Advent 13
    Fourth Sunday In Advent 15

Christmas
    Christmas Eve/Day 18
    Christmas Day (Additional Lections) 20
    Christmas Day (Additional Lections) 22
    First Sunday After Christmas 24
    Second Sunday After Christmas 26
    New Year's Eve/Day 29

Epiphany
    Epiphany of the Lord 31
    First Sunday After Epiphany 33
    Second Sunday After Epiphany 35
    Third Sunday After Epiphany 37
    Fourth Sunday After Epiphany 39
    Fifth Sunday After Epiphany 41
    Sixth Sunday After Epiphany 43
    Seventh Sunday After Epiphany 45
    Eighth Sunday After Epiphany 47
    Ninth Sunday After Epiphany 49
    Last Sunday After Epiphany (Transfiguration) 51

Lent
    Ash Wednesday 53
    First Sunday In Lent 55
    Second Sunday In Lent 57
    Third Sunday In Lent 59
    Fourth Sunday In Lent 61
    Fifth Sunday In Lent 63
    Sixth Sunday In Lent 66
    Maundy Thursday 70

Easter

Easter Sunday	72
Second Sunday Of Easter	74
Third Sunday Of Easter	76
Fourth Sunday Of Easter	78
Fifth Sunday Of Easter	80
Sixth Sunday Of Easter	82
Ascension Day	84
Seventh Sunday In Easter	86

Pentecost

Pentecost	88
Trinity Sunday	90
Proper 4	92
Proper 5	94
Proper 6	96
Proper 7	98
Proper 8	101
Proper 9	103
Proper 10	105
Proper 11	107
Proper 12	109
Proper 13	111
Proper 14	113
Proper 15	115
Proper 16	117
Proper 17	119
Proper 18	121
Proper 19	123
Proper 20	126
Proper 21	128
Proper 22	130
Proper 23	132
Proper 24	134
Proper 25	136
Proper 26	138
Proper 27	140
Proper 28	142
Christ The King	144
All Saints'	146
Thanksgiving	148
Index of the Scripture Passages	150
A note concerning lectionaries and calendars	154

AN ORDER OF WORSHIP

Prelude
*Call to Worship
Hymn of Praise, Psalm or Spiritual Song
*Prayer of Confession
*Declaration of Pardon and Exhortation
The Peace
First Lesson
*Psalm
Gloria Patri
Second Lesson
Gospel
*Prayer of the Day
Hymn
Sermon
Creed
*Prayer of Thanksgiving
Prayers of Intercession
Offering
*Prayer of Dedication
Hymn
The Benediction

* These parts of the service are spelled out for each Sunday of Year B in the pages of this book.

If you do not have this book in the pew, at least reproduce the Psalm for responsive or antiphonal reading. The Prayer of Confession and the Declaration of Pardon should also be reproduced for congregational reading and the Prayer of the Day. For maximum participation, the Prayer of Thanksgiving and the Prayer of Dedication may also be printed out.

FIRST SUNDAY IN ADVENT

Isaiah 64:1-9   Psalm 80:1-7, 17-19
1 Corinthians 1:3-9   Mark 13:24-37

• CALL TO WORSHIP
Wait expectantly for our Lord Jesus Christ to reveal himself. He will keep you firm to the end, without reproach on the Day of our Lord Jesus. It is God in person, who called you to share in the life of the Son, Jesus Christ our Lord; and God keeps faith.

• PRAYER OF CONFESSION
God of many names, by what name shall we call you? Our question rises out of some confusion, not only about who you are, but about who we are, for you have declared yourself to be our kin, One who has ransomed us. In some ways you are like a permissive parent, who allows us enough room to get ourselves into trouble when we follow undisciplined instincts. Too often we are more like people who claim no affinity to you than like a people who bear your name. Forgive our tendency to slough off responsibility for our decision. Excuse the incompleteness of many of our confessions. We trust you still because of Jesus Christ, your Son. Amen.

• DECLARATION OF GOD'S FORGIVENESS
Hear the Good News! God has given you grace and peace in Christ Jesus, and enriched you with many good gifts. Friends, believe the Good News. In Jesus Christ, we are forgiven.

• EXHORTATION
Be alert and watchful, for no one knows when the Son of Man will come with great power and glory. Do not neglect to finish the work he has given you to do.

• PRAYER OF THE DAY
Divine Timekeeper, keep us alert by the chimes of the times that whether Christ comes again, at dawn or high noon, in the evening or at midnight, we will be ready to welcome his return, enabled by the Spirit to show that our house is in order and that we are honored by his coming. Amen.

• PRAYER OF THANKSGIVING
God of grace, Child of peace, Spirit of truth, we join with all the members of the church everywhere in the world in giving thanks for all the gifts you have given to enrich the whole church. Though each of us do not have all

gifts, there is no needful gift lacking to your church through the talents you have distributed among us. In Jesus Christ you have given us life and truth, grace and peace. Through days of persecution and days of plenty, you have sustained the church and kept it firm in expectation of the return of the Lord, Jesus Christ. *Your favor is unmerited. Your peace is undeserved. Your truth is beyond our comprehension. We celebrate your generosity, in Jesus Christ. Amen.*

• PRAYER OF DEDICATION
Lord of the church, you are not enriched by our gifts but enable us to share our talents for the enrichment of the whole congregation, young and old and middle aged. We present ourselves to be useful to each other and to you. Amen.

• PSALM 80:1-7, 17-19
Give ear, O Shepherd of Israel,
you who lead Joseph like a flock!
You who are enthroned upon the cherubim,
shine forth before Ephraim and Benjamin and Manasseh.
Stir up your might,
and come to save us!
Restore us, O God;
let your face shine, that we may be saved.
O LORD God of hosts,
how long will you be angry with your people's prayers?
You have fed them with the bread of tears,
and given them tears to drink in full measure.
You make us the scorn of our neighbors;
our enemies laugh among themselves.
Restore us, O God of hosts;
let your face shine, that we may be saved.
But let your hand be upon the one at your right hand,
the one whom you made strong for yourself.
Then we will never turn back from you;
give us life, and we will call on your name.
Restore us, O LORD God of hosts;
let your face shine, that we may be saved.

SECOND SUNDAY IN ADVENT

Isaiah 40:1-11   Psalm 85:1-2, 8-13
2 Peter 3:8-15a   Mark 1:1-8

• CALL TO WORSHIP
Hear the words of the Lord. Are they not words of peace, peace to his people and to his loyal servants and to all who turn and trust in him?

• PRAYER OF CONFESSION
God of the first day, God of today, God of the last day, we admit that we are more frightened by the threat of a nuclear accident or a nuclear war than we are hopeful for a new heaven and earth. It is like our apprehension of major surgery, an unpleasant experience, but one that can bring about the condition in which healing can take place. We may be fatalistic and feel powerless to change unjust institutions that provoke and promote war. Forgive our reluctance to look for the new day and to work for justice and peace with patience, repentance, and perseverance, whatever the disappointments and delays. Baptize us with the Holy Spirit according to the gospel of Jesus Christ, your Son. Amen.

• DECLARATION OF GOD'S FORGIVENESS
Hear the Good News! God has forgiven your guilt and put away all your sins. Friends, believe the Good News! In Jesus Christ, we are forgiven.

• EXHORTATION
Prepare a road for the Lord through the barren places of our common life. Clear a highway for God across the fruitless areas of our history.

• PRAYER OF THE DAY
Jesus Christ, Son of God, since you have walked in our shoes, enable us by the same Holy Spirit of our baptism to proclaim the good news and prepare the way for your coming again so that you may be surrounded by people from all earth's cities and countrysides. Amen.

• PRAYER OF THANKSGIVING
Saving God, loving Christ, baptizing Spirit, hear our thanksgiving for all who have paved the way for your good news to reach us. We admire the bold preaching of the prophets and apostles. We appreciate the work of scholars and translators in preparing a written text for us to read. We are grateful for the printers and binders that make Bibles for us and for all who help us to read and understand the Word of God written. Most of all we

thank you that your saving and forgiving love was embodied in Jesus of Nazareth, the great good Shepherd who has gathered his flock into the Church. For past deliverance, for present comfort, for future promise we give you thanks, faithful God.   Amen.

- **PRAYER OF DEDICATION**
We worship you, loving and faithful Lord, by the presentation of these tokens of our prosperity and the yield of our work. Use us and our offerings to spread the gospel of Jesus Christ.   Amen.

- **PSALM 85:1-2, 8-13**
LORD, you were favorable to your land;
you restored the fortunes of Jacob.
You forgave the iniquity of your people;
you pardoned all their sin.
Let me hear what God the LORD will speak,
for he will speak peace to his people,
to his faithful, to those who turn to him in their hearts.
Surely his salvation is at hand for those who fear him,
that his glory may dwell in our land.
Steadfast love and faithfulness will meet;
righteousness and peace will kiss each other.
Faithfulness will spring up from the ground,
and righteousness will look down from the sky.
The LORD will give what is good,
and our land will yield its increase.
Righteousness will go before him,
and will make a path for his steps.

THIRD SUNDAY IN ADVENT

Isaiah 61:1-4, 8-11 Luke 1:46b-55 or Psalm 126
1 Thessalonians 5:16-24 John 1:6-8, 19-28

• **CALL TO WORSHIP**
Tell out the greatness of the Lord. Rejoice in God your Savior.

• **PRAYER OF CONFESSION**
Infinite Parent, Incarnate Offspring, Inclusive Spirit, in Jesus Christ you have experienced our humanity. We admit that we are not yet holy in spirit, soul and body. Our worship is not always wholehearted. Our hearts and minds are often arrogant, prejudiced, unchangeable. Our bodies are too prone to rule us, and bad habits jeopardize our health. Forgive our faults and fulfill your promise through the communion of the Holy Spirit that we may be faultless when our Lord Jesus comes, to the glory of your great name. Amen.

• **DECLARATION OF GOD'S FORGIVENESS**
Hear the Good News! God's mercy is sure from generation to generation, and firm in the promise to our ancestors that God will not forget to show mercy to their children's children. Friends, believe the Good News! In Jesus Christ, we are forgiven.

• **EXHORTATION**
Be always joyful. Pray continually. Give thanks whatever happens; for this is what God in Christ wills for you.

• **PRAYER OF THE DAY**
Outgoing God, gift us again with the Holy Spirit that we may make way for you to the humble with good news, to the captives with promises of release, to the bereaved with the comfort of beauty and new gladness, to the brokenhearted with tender, loving care, and to the oppressed with the promise of eventual justice. Lord God, make righteousness and praise blossom before all nations. Amen.

• **PRAYER OF THANKSGIVING**
Hallowed be your name, mighty God, hallowed be your name, merciful God. Hallowed be your name, active God, you side with the humble rather than the proud, with the poor rather than the rich, with the powerless rather than the powerful. You come into our world in Mary's child, Jesus of Nazareth, the Son nearest your heart, full of grace and truth. Thanks

be given to you always, in Hebrew and Greek and English and in every language of the universe. Amen.

• **PRAYER OF DEDICATION**
God who promised to come, has come, and has promised to come again, we are preparing ourselves for your return and offer our gifts and ourselves to make the way straight for Jesus Christ our Lord. Amen.

• **PSALM 126**
When the LORD restored the fortunes of Zion,
we were like those who dream.
Then our mouth was filled with laughter,
and our tongue with shouts of joy;
*then it was said among the nations,
"The LORD has done great things for them."*
*The LORD has done great things for us,
and we rejoiced.*
Restore our fortunes, O LORD,
like the watercourses in the Negeb.
May those who sow in tears reap with shouts of joy.
*Those who go out weeping, bearing the seed for sowing,
shall come home with shouts of joy, carrying their sheaves.*

(or)

• **LUKE 1:46b-55**
"My soul magnifies the Lord,
and my spirit rejoices in God my Savior,
for he has looked with favor on the lowliness of his servant.
Surely, from now on all generations will call me blessed;
*for the Mighty One has done great things for me,
and holy is his name.*
His mercy is for those who fear him
from generation to generation.
He has shown strength with his arm;
he has scattered the proud in the thoughts of their hearts.
He has brought down the powerful from their thrones,
and lifted up the lowly;
he has filled the hungry with good things,
and sent the rich away empty.
He has helped his servant Israel, in remembrance of his mercy,
*according to the promise he made to our ancestors,
to Abraham and to his descendants forever."*

FOURTH SUNDAY IN ADVENT

2 Samuel 7:1-11,16　　　　　Luke 1:47-55 or Psalm 89:1-4, 19-26
Romans 16:25-27　　　　　　　　　　　　　　　　Luke 1:26-38

• **CALL TO WORSHIP**
Happy are the people who have learned to give acclaim to God, and who walk in the light of the Lord's presence.

• **PRAYER OF CONFESSION**
God to humanity descending, Man to God ascended, God to all condescending, you send prophets to lead adulterous royalty to repentance and angels to innocent, common folk to direct them in your service. Forgive any unwillingness we have shown to do your will, any reticence to proclaim the good news of Jesus Christ, any doubt that your promised kingdom will fully come and will not fail. We have not been prepared to serve you at the risk of personal reputation or at hazard of private wealth. Have mercy on us, for the sake of Jesus Christ, who served your purpose without reservation. Amen.

• **DECLARATION OF GOD'S FORGIVENESS**
Hear the Good News! The Divine secret kept in silence for long ages has been disclosed through the proclamation of Jesus Christ and the prophetic scriptures made known to all nations. Friends, believe the Good News! In Jesus Christ, we are forgiven.

• **EXHORTATION**
Come in faith and obedience to God through Jesus Christ that the presence of the Holy Spirit may make your standing sure, to the glory of God.

• **PRAYER OF THE DAY**
God of all life, grant to us who are called to parenthood your Holy Spirit to develop our self-control, that in begetting and conceiving, we may give birth to holy children, dedicated to you by their baptism and nurtured in your service through our family life, by Jesus Christ, Son of the Most High. Amen.

• **PRAYER OF THANKSGIVING**
We will sing the story of your love, O God, forever. We will proclaim your faithfulness to all generations. You declare your true love in covenants made with humble nations. You reassure the lowly person of your gracious favor. You call young and old alike to serve your purposes and complete

your loving designs. We celebrate the motherhood of young Mary and old Elizabeth. We mark again with great joy the birth of the Son of God, the son of David, the son of Mary, Jesus of Nazareth, known as Joseph's son. We worship you, God the sender. We worship you, Jesus, the sent One, Son of the most high and son of the most humble. We worship you, Holy Spirit, God in touch with our humanity. Glory be to God in heaven and earth. Amen.

• **PRAYER OF DEDICATION**
The most majestic music is not an adequate gift of adoration to you and yet you hear the simplest song. The most precious gift is beneath your notice and yet you receive whatever is given out of the deepest poverty. Let our gifts and our lives be worthy of you as they can be only in the grace of our Lord Jesus Christ and the enabling Spirit. Amen.

• **PSALM 89:1-4, 19-26**
I declare that your steadfast love is established forever;
your faithfulness is as firm as the heavens.
You said, "I have made a covenant with my chosen one,
I have sworn to my servant David:
'I will establish your descendants forever,
and build your throne for all generations.' "
Then you spoke in a vision to your faithful one,
and said: "I have set the crown on one who is mighty,
I have exalted one chosen from the people.
I have found my servant David;
with my holy oil I have anointed him;
my hand shall always remain with him;
my arm also shall strengthen him.
The enemy shall not outwit him,
the wicked shall not humble him.
I will crush his foes before him
and strike down those who hate him.
My faithfulness and steadfast love shall be with him;
and in my name his horn shall be exalted.
I will set his hand on the sea
and his right hand on the rivers.
He shall cry to me, 'You are my Father,
my God, and the Rock of my salvation!' "
(or)

• **LUKE 1:46b-55**
"My soul magnifies the Lord,
and my spirit rejoices in God my Savior,
for he has looked with favor on the lowliness of his servant.
Surely, from now on all generations will call me blessed;
for the Mighty One has done great things for me,
and holy is his name.
His mercy is for those who fear him
from generation to generation.
He has shown strength with his arm;
he has scattered the proud in the thoughts of their hearts.
He has brought down the powerful from their thrones,
and lifted up the lowly;
he has filled the hungry with good things,
and sent the rich away empty.
He has helped his servant Israel, in remembrance of his mercy,
according to the promise he made to our ancestors,
to Abraham and to his descendants forever."

CHRISTMAS EVE / DAY

Isaiah 9:2-7　　　　　　　　　　　　　　　　　　　　Psalm 96
Titus 2:11-14　　　　　　　　　　　　　　　　Luke 2:1-14, (15-20)

• CALL TO WORSHIP
Silence, everyone, in the presence of God, who has come out of the sanctuary of heaven.

• PRAYER OF CONFESSION
God of all worlds, ours seems at times like an abandoned one. We share in its sin, its darkness and its despair. We feel that you have left us alone to find our own way out of the mess we have made of things. We have forgotten that the world was created by you, re-visited by you in Jesus Christ, and is still yours, a dwelling place of your choice for your Spirit. Forgive the belief that you are nowhere, that forgets that you are now here, in the Spirit of Jesus Christ. Amen.

• DECLARATION OF GOD'S FORGIVENESS
Hear the Good News! The Lord has come, and is coming again. Let the peace of God keep guard over your hearts and your thoughts, in Christ Jesus. Friends, believe the Good News! In Jesus Christ, we are forgiven.

• EXHORTATION
The Lord is near. Have no anxiety, but in everything make your requests known to God in prayer and petition with thanksgiving.

• PRAYER OF THE DAY
Child of Bethlehem, Man of Nazareth, Christ of God, with Mary we treasure the stories of your birth and ponder over these things. May the celebration of your birth, both in this place and in our social circles, bring glory and praise to your name. Amen.

• PRAYER OF THANKSGIVING
Shepherd of Israel, Lamb of God, Keeper of Christ's flock, with Bethlehem shepherds of old, we come to see what has happened and consider what has been made known to us. We rejoice in the birth of this child Jesus who embodies both the good Shepherd and the Lamb of God that takes away the sin of the world. For his obedience to your saving purpose we are thankful. That you become involved in the sin and suffering of our world, we are astonished. That you continue to draw us together as your flock by the Spirit we are comforted. Amen.

- **PRAYER OF DEDICATION**
Not often enough, O God, do we offer you the gift of our silence, in adoration, in attentiveness, in anticipation of your directions. Receive us in this solemn moment, and in such times of silence as we find for you in the days to come. Amen.

- **PSALM 96**
O sing to the LORD a new song;
sing to the LORD, all the earth.
Sing to the LORD, bless his name;
tell of his salvation from day to day.
Declare his glory among the nations,
his marvelous works among all the peoples.
For great is the LORD,
and greatly to be praised;
he is to be revered above all gods.
For all the gods of the peoples are idols,
but the LORD made the heavens.
Honor and majesty are before him;
strength and beauty are in his sanctuary.
Ascribe to the LORD, O families of the peoples,
ascribe to the LORD glory and strength.
Ascribe to the LORD the glory due his name;
bring an offering, and come into his courts.
Worship the LORD in holy splendor;
tremble before him, all the earth.
Say among the nations, "The LORD is king!
The world is firmly established;
it shall never be moved.
He will judge the peoples with equity."
Let the heavens be glad,
and let the earth rejoice;
let the sea roar, and all that fills it;
let the field exult, and everything in it.
Then shall all the trees of the forest sing for joy before the LORD;
for he is coming, for he is coming to judge the earth.
He will judge the world with righteousness,
and the peoples with his truth.

CHRISTMAS DAY
(Additional Lections)

Isaiah 62:6-12   Psalm 97
Titus 3:4-7   Luke 2:(1-7), 8-20

• **CALL TO WORSHIP**
I have Good News for you: there is great joy coming to the whole people. Today in the city of David a deliverer has been born to you — the Messiah, the Christ.

• **PRAYER OF CONFESSION**
God of the gospel, whose glory brightens the night sky on Christmas eve, and the birth of whose Son in Bethlehem brings the dawn of a new day, hear our prayers for forgiveness and mercy. Pardon us if we have made idols of what are only symbols of the coming of Jesus, if traditional practice rather than the reality of the coming of Jesus Christ, has defined the meaning of today. We can appeal to your kindness and generosity, not because of any good deeds of our own, but because of our salvation through the water of baptism and the renewing power of the Holy Spirit. By your grace, Jesus Christ is our Savior. Amen.

• **DECLARATION OF GOD'S FORGIVENESS**
Hear the Good News! God in highest heaven grants peace on earth to all on whom rests the favor of the Most High. Friends, believe the Good News! In Jesus Christ, we are forgiven.

• **EXHORTATION**
Raise a signal to all people. This is God's proclamation to earth's farthest bounds.

• **PRAYER OF THE DAY**
Exalted One, having received the good news of Jesus Christ with great joy we would be sent like the shepherds to astonish others with the story of Jesus and the meaning of our salvation through his grace. Amen.

• **PRAYER OF THANKSGIVING**
God in highest heaven, we give you thanks for the sending of Jesus Christ into our world to be a gift of peace, a person of peace, a prince of peace. Christ most lowly, we give thanks for your humble birth and gracious life, for salvation and the hope of eternal life. Spirit most holy, we thank you for the water of rebirth and the renewal of the Spirit thus signified, by

which we are saved, being justified by the grace of our Lord Jesus Christ.
All glory be ascribed to you, God, Giving, Coming, Renewing. Amen.

• **PRAYER OF DEDICATION**
Holy Child of God and of Mary Virgin, heaven and earth are your homes, temple and stable are hallowed by your presence. We bring our gifts to you so that the good news of peace may continue to sound in earth and heaven, echoed by human voices, the voice of your church. Amen.

• **PSALM 97:1-12**
The LORD is king! Let the earth rejoice;
let the many coastlands be glad!
Clouds and thick darkness are all around him;
righteousness and justice are the foundation of his throne.
Fire goes before him,
and consumes his adversaries on every side.
His lightnings light up the world;
the earth sees and trembles.
The mountains melt like wax before the LORD,
before the Lord of all the earth.
The heavens proclaim his righteousness;
and all the peoples behold his glory.
All worshipers of images are put to shame,
those who make their boast in worthless idols;
all gods bow down before him
Zion hears and is glad,
and the towns of Judah rejoice,
because of your judgments, O God.
For you, O LORD, are most high over all the earth;
you are exalted far above all gods.
The LORD loves those who hate evil;
he guards the lives of his faithful;
he rescues them from the hand of the wicked.
Light dawns for the righteous,
and joy for the upright in heart.
Rejoice in the LORD, O you righteous,
and give thanks to his holy name!

CHRISTMAS DAY
(Additional Lections)

Isaiah 52:7-10   Psalm 98
Hebrews 1:1-4, (5-12)   John 1:1-14

• CALL TO WORSHIP
Receive Jesus Christ, who is the Word made flesh, and who has come to dwell among us, full of grace and truth.

• PRAYER OF CONFESSION
True God, Gracious God, we are still enticed to idolatry. We are fascinated by glamorous stars. We are taken in by false propaganda. We are frightened by the threats of the politically and economically powerful. We lose confidence in your pledge to preserve the lives of your saints. We forget that you love those who hate evil and resist it. Forgive our misplaced confidence, our faith in the wrong powers. Restore our joy in the gentle qualities of truth and grace made personal in Jesus Christ. Amen.

• DECLARATION OF GOD'S FORGIVENESS
Hear the Good News! In Christ our release is secured and our sins are forgiven through the shedding of his blood. In receiving God's only Son, you have been received as a child of God. Friends, believe the Good News! In Jesus Christ, we are forgiven.

• EXHORTATION
Bear witness to the light of grace and truth that you have seen in Jesus Christ. There are others who have not yet recognized him as the real light that enlightens everyone coming into the world.

• PRAYER OF THE DAY
Mender of our broken world, enable us as members of your family to be cooperative agents in the restoration of the unity of all things in Christ, all things in heaven and earth. Then will all the earth be glad and the stars sing for joy. Amen.

• PRAYER OF THANKSGIVING
We hail your coming, invisible Sovereign, incarnate Prince, powerful Spirit. We rejoice with apostles who lived in the historic days of Jesus Christ, your Son, and with prophets who anticipated that day. With all your earthly realm we join our voices in praise of the glory revealed in

Jesus Christ. We run with the good news of the reunification of all things around your beloved. We praise you for all the spiritual blessings that you give us, here and hereafter. Amen.

• **PRAYER OF DEDICATION**
We renew our allegiance to you, God's Child, acknowledging our adoption as your brothers and sisters. We pledge our resources and ourselves, that the light shall shine on and the darkness never overwhelm it. Amen.

• **PSALM 98**
O sing to the LORD a new song, for he has done marvelous things.
His right hand and his holy arm have gotten him victory.
The LORD has made known his victory;
he has revealed his vindication in the sight of the nations.
He has remembered his steadfast love and faithfulness
    to the house of Israel.
All the ends of the earth have seen the victory of our God.
Make a joyful noise to the LORD, all the earth;
break forth into joyous song and sing praises.
Sing praises to the LORD with the lyre,
with the lyre and the sound of melody.
With trumpets and the sound of the horn
make a joyful noise before the King, the LORD.
Let the sea roar, and all that fills it;
the world and those who live in it.
Let the floods clap their hands;
let the hills sing together for joy
at the presence of the LORD,
for he is coming to judge the earth.
He will judge the world with righteousness,
and the peoples with equity.

FIRST SUNDAY AFTER CHRISTMAS

Isaiah 61:10-62:3 Psalm 148
Galatians 4:4-7 Luke 2:22-40

• CALL TO WORSHIP
Let us rejoice in God with all our hearts for our Savior robes us with salvation like a garment and clothes us in integrity like a cloak.

• PRAYER OF CONFESSION
Spirit of God, given to guide us to the place of prayer and to open our minds and hearts to what we should know, we confess that we do not always heed your bidding and often miss seeing what you have shown to those who have been obedient to your prompting. Forgive the stubbornness that resists learning, not admitting our need to know nor confessing the sins we seek to hide. Amen.

• DECLARATION OF GOD'S FORGIVENESS
Hear the Good News! God sent his own Son, born of a woman, born under the law, to purchase freedom for the slaves of the law so that we might have the dignity of God's heirs. Friends, believe the Good News! In Jesus Christ, we are forgiven.

• EXHORTATION
As God's, children grow in wisdom and stature and in favor with God and your neighbors.

• PRAYER OF THE DAY
Eternal Spirit, so guide us in worship and in learning that we may experience your salvation and speak with confidence of your grace through Jesus Christ. Amen.

• PRAYER OF THANKSGIVING
Eternal God, historic Christ, timeless Spirit, we rejoice in the salvation that you have planned and are fulfilling in the birth of Christ Jesus and in the continuing work of the Spirit in the church. You have freed us who have believed and are liberating those who are coming to faith in Jesus Christ. You bring goodness and beauty to flower in neighborhoods and nations. All praise be given to you, O God. Amen.

• **PRAYER OF DEDICATION**
As in their poverty the holy family brought their simple offerings to the temple, O God, so we bring our offerings in thanksgiving for the salvation you have brought us through Jesus Christ, your Son, our Savior. Amen.

• **PSALM 148**
Praise the LORD! Praise the LORD from the heavens;
praise him in the heights!
Praise him, all his angels;
praise him, all his host!
Praise him, sun and moon;
praise him, all you shining stars!
Praise him, you highest heavens,
and you waters above the heavens!
Let them praise the name of the LORD,
for he commanded and they were created.
He established them forever and ever;
he fixed their bounds, which cannot be passed.
Praise the LORD from the earth,
you sea monsters and all deeps,
fire and hail, snow and frost,
stormy wind fulfilling his command!
Mountains and all hills,
fruit trees and all cedars!
Wild animals and all cattle,
creeping things and flying birds!
Kings of the earth and all peoples,
princes and all rulers of the earth!
Young men and women alike,
old and young together!
Let them praise the name of the LORD,
for his name alone is exalted;
his glory is above earth and heaven.
He has raised up a horn for his people,
praise for all his faithful,
for the people of Israel who are close to him. Praise the LORD!

SECOND SUNDAY AFTER CHRISTMAS

Jeremiah 31:7-14 Psalm 147:12-20
or Sirach 24:1-12 or Wisdom of Solomon 10:15-21
Ephesians 1:3-14 John 1:(1-9), 10-18

- **CALL TO WORSHIP (Responsively)**
Sing out your praises and say,
God has saved his people.
See how the Savior brings them from the end of the earth,
The blind and lame among them,
Women with child
And women in labor, a great company.
Young men and old shall rejoice,
Then shall the girl show her joy in the dance.
God turns their mourning into gladness,
And gives them joy to outdo their sorrow.

- **PRAYER OF CONFESSION**
All glorious God, paternal, fraternal, maternal, *though we have faith in Jesus Christ, and love towards your people yet we are not without blemish in your sight, not full of love, wisdom, and other spiritual blessings you still have available for us. Our love is not as inclusive as yours, and there is much we need to learn. Give us clearer vision of all that we are meant to be, so that by becoming fulfilled, we may increase the glory that is properly revealed in Jesus Christ, your beloved. Amen.*

- **DECLARATION OF GOD'S FORGIVENESS**
Hear the Good News! The liberator has come to free us from all proud pretenses. The Christ has come in Jesus of Nazareth to show us the undeserved favor of God. Friends, believe the Good News! In Jesus Christ, we are forgiven.

- **EXHORTATION**
Accept the limitations of your own knowledge. Have reverence for the wisdom of the Creator. Be thankful for his love in Christ and for a humble place in his house.

- **PRAYER OF THE DAY**
Available God, whatever our age, whether married or single, make us sensitive to what you are doing and about to do, that we may not miss the

excitement of being a part of the living history that you are writing, through Jesus Christ. Amen.

- **PRAYER OF THANKSGIVING**
We give thanks, God of Job and Jeremiah, David's Lord, Anna's Christ, Luke's savior, that we have found your house in many places. We have found places of prayer with the swallows and the sparrows. We have sung your praise in a quiet circle under the stars. We have enjoyed the choir of many voices and the joyous sounds of musical instruments and found inspiration and refreshment. Along our pilgrim way you provide the cup that sustains both soul and body. We are happy when we trust in you. Amen.

- **PRAYER OF DEDICATION**
God of all places, many of us return to this place again and again, expecting spiritual refreshment and growth in grace. Bless all that we do to make this a place of renewal for all who will come to Jesus Christ. Amen.

- **PSALM 147:12-20**
Praise the LORD, O Jerusalem!
Praise your God, O Zion!
For he strengthens the bars of your gates;
he blesses your children within you.
He grants peace within your borders;
he fills you with the finest of wheat.
He sends out his command to the earth;
his word runs swiftly.
He gives snow like wool;
he scatters frost like ashes.
He hurls down hail like crumbs
— who can stand before his cold?
He sends out his word, and melts them;
he makes his wind blow, and the waters flow.
He declares his word to Jacob,
his statutes and ordinances to Israel.
He has not dealt thus with any other nation;
they do not know his ordinances.
Praise the LORD!

(or)

• **WISDOM 10:15-21**
A holy people and blameless race
wisdom delivered from a nation of oppressors.
She entered the soul of a servant of the Lord,
and withstood dread kings with wonders and signs.
She gave to holy people the reward of their labors;
she guided them along a marvelous way,
and became a shelter to them by day,
and a starry flame through the night.
She brought them over the Red Sea,
and led them through deep waters;
but she drowned their enemies,
and cast them up from the depth of the sea.
Therefore the righteous plundered the ungodly;
they sang hymns, O Lord, to your holy name,
and praised with one accord your defending hand;
for wisdom opened the mouths of those who were mute,
and made the tongues of infants speak clearly.

NEW YEAR'S EVE/DAY

Ecclesiastes 3:1-13　　　　　　　　　　　　　　　Psalm 8
Revelation 21:1-6a　　　　　　　　　　　　Matthew 25:31-46

• **CALL TO WORSHIP**
Worship God, our Sovereign, with reverence for the majesty of God's name in all the earth!

• **PRAYER OF CONFESSION**
God before time, God in our time, God Eternal, you mark our days and years for what we have experienced and what we have learned. You give us time to develop characters shaped by joy and sorrow. We do not always learn willingly and change our ways to follow the way of Jesus Christ. Pardon our stubbornness and give us further time to learn and improve our times for the sake of your perfect Son, Jesus Christ. Amen.

• **DECLARATION OF GOD'S FORGIVENESS**
Hear the Good News! We have been given time to reconsider our ways and to prepare ourselves for the day of judgement yet to come. Friends, believe the Good News! In Jesus Christ, we are forgiven.

• **EXHORTATION**
Feed the hungry; give drink to the thirsty; welcome strangers; clothe the naked; visit the sick and prisoners; you will be ready for the day of reckoning.

• **PRAYER OF THE DAY**
Open our eyes, Divine Healer, that we may see your face in the faces of the poor, the sick and the prisoner and in caring for them give homage to you, our Savior and Friend. Amen.

• **PRAYER OF THANKSGIVING**
Unchanging God, Contemporary Christ, ageless Spirit, for all that you teach us in the course of life we give thanks. We are grateful for what you provide for us to eat and drink and for the pleasures of meaningful work. We enjoy times of recreation and love making. We anticipate the end of hate and war and want. We look for the defaced to be removed with the coming of the new heaven and earth in which there is love perfected, peace with justice and plenty shared generously. Hasten the time of healing when we can live together without fear or misunderstanding in your new heaven and earth under the banner of love. Glory to God, drying tears, ending suffering, sharing glory. Amen.

• PRAYER OF DEDICATION
God of the past year, God of today, God of this new year, receive the offerings that we bring and the service we pledge not only for your worship in this place but for ministry to those in need; for Christ's sake. Amen.

• PSALM 8
O LORD, our Sovereign, how majestic is your name in all the earth!
You have set your glory above the heavens.
Out of the mouths of babes and infants you have founded a bulwark because of your foes,
to silence the enemy and the avenger.
When I look at your heavens, the work of your fingers,
the moon and the stars that you have established;
what are human beings that you are mindful of them,
mortals that you care for them?
Yet you have made them a little lower than God,
and crowned them with glory and honor.
You have given them dominion over the works of your hands;
you have put all things under their feet,
all sheep and oxen, and also the beasts of the field,
the birds of the air, and the fish of the sea,
whatever passes along the paths of the seas.
O LORD, our Sovereign, how majestic is your name in all the earth!

EPIPHANY OF THE LORD

Isaiah 60:1-6   Psalm 72:1-7, 10-14
Ephesians 3:1-12   Matthew 2:1-12

- **CALL TO WORSHIP**
Give homage to the Christ. Bring him your treasures and offer him your gifts.

- **PRAYER OF CONFESSION**
God of justice and peace, for some of us it is difficult to determine whether we are among the oppressors or the oppressed. We declare our belief in justice, but are concerned mostly for our own rights and not always for the rights of others. Your anointed One came to help those who are needy and to give judgment for the suffering. Though we are loyal to him in principle we are not always with him in practice. Forgive such hypocrisy, for Jesus' sake. Amen.

- **DECLARATION OF GOD'S FORGIVENESS**
Hear the Good News! Through Jesus Christ, we who are not Jews may share with them God's promise. Friends, believe the Good News! In Jesus Christ, we are forgiven.

- **EXHORTATION**
Pass on the Good News. It is no longer a secret to be kept from anyone. The whole human race may be part of the body of Christ, His Church.

- **PRAYER OF THE DAY**
Give us the courage, divine Ruler, if ever we must choose between obedience to earthly or heavenly monarch, to be obedient to the heavenly vision. Free us from being yoked with any oppressor, that we may be among the nations that march toward your light, shining in Jesus Christ. Amen.

- **PRAYER OF THANKSGIVING**
We rejoice with the prophet, your prophet, O God, who sees the vision of the new Jerusalem. We look for the day when the city of God on earth will be the gathering of the world's children in a city of light. Though there is darkness covering the earth and dark night the nations, the glory, your glory, shall appear. To your presence will march the nations, and rulers to your rising with the radiance of the sun. In such visions that lighten our darkness, we are overjoyed, like the Magi in seeing the star. Amen.

• PRAYER OF DEDICATION
Gold, frankincense and myrrh are not our gifts, but what we have is yours to use, O Christ, in the support of your church and in the service of others. Amen.

• PSALM 72:1-7,10-14
Give the king your justice, O God,
and your righteousness to a king's son.
May he judge your people with righteousness,
and your poor with justice.
May the mountains yield prosperity for the people,
and the hills, in righteousness.
May he defend the cause of the poor of the people,
give deliverance to the needy, and crush the oppressor.
May he live while the sun endures,
and as long as the moon, throughout all generations.
May he be like rain that falls on the mown grass,
like showers that water the earth.
In his days may righteousness flourish and peace abound,
until the moon is no more.
May the kings of Tarshish and of the isles render him tribute,
may the kings of Sheba and Seba bring gifts.
May all kings fall down before him,
all nations give him service.
For he delivers the needy when they call,
the poor and those who have no helper.
He has pity on the weak and the needy,
and saves the lives of the needy.
From oppression and violence he redeems their life;
and precious is their blood in his sight.

FIRST SUNDAY AFTER EPIPHANY

Genesis 1:1-5   Psalm 29
Acts 19:1-7   Mark 1:4-11

- **CALL TO WORSHIP**
Ascribe to the Anointed the glory due to Christ's name; bow down to the Messiah in the splendor of holiness.

- **PRAYER OF CONFESSION**
Creator of what is good, Christ for sinners, Spirit of restoration, we require the baptism of repentance but might not be ready to confess it except that your obedient Son, Jesus, identified himself with us in our sins and showed us your gracious forgiveness signified in the cleansing and refreshing waters of our baptism. Forgive any lack of candidness in our confessions. We need to learn more thorough-going honesty before you, ALL-TRUTH, ALL-LEARNING, ALL-LIFE. Amen.

- **DECLARATION OF GOD'S FORGIVENESS**
Hear the Good News! The Holy Spirit is given to us as we put our trust in the name of Jesus Christ our Savior. Friends, believe the Good News! In Jesus Christ, we are forgiven.

- **EXHORTATION**
Make your own preparations for the coming of Christ and be ready to give a royal welcome at the return of the Scion of heaven and earth.

- **PRAYER OF THE DAY**
Exalted Parent, as you acknowledged your beloved Son, Jesus, so graciously adopt us as your children being pleased in what your Spirit will yet accomplish in making us more like him to the glory of our family name in Christ. Amen.

- **PRAYER OF THANKSGIVING**
Eternal Sovereign, Thunderous Voice, Peace-giving Spirit, we hear the echo of your voice in the majesty of your Creation and the sob of your grief in what we have thoughtlessly despoiled. Let our thanksgiving be not only the praise we can give to the beauty of what you created but the activities we undertake to restore what has been uglified by rapacity and waste. In the restoration of what has been spoiled may we sense the presence of the Spirit of peace and joy. Amen.

- **PRAYER OF DEDICATION**
Powerful Creator, Humble Savior, Renewing Spirit, renew in us the generous nature which is your image in which we were created in the beginning that the beauty of the world and the order of church may be advanced in every generation. Amen.

- **PSALM 29:1-11**
Ascribe to the LORD, O heavenly beings,
ascribe to the LORD glory and strength.
Ascribe to the LORD the glory of his name;
worship the LORD in holy splendor.
The voice of the LORD is over the waters;
the God of glory thunders, the LORD, over mighty waters.
The voice of the LORD is powerful;
the voice of the LORD is full of majesty.
The voice of the LORD breaks the cedars;
the LORD breaks the cedars of Lebanon.
He makes Lebanon skip like a calf,
and Sirion like a young wild ox.
The voice of the LORD flashes forth flames of fire.
The voice of the LORD shakes the wilderness;
the LORD shakes the wilderness of Kadesh.
The voice of the LORD causes the oaks to whirl,
and strips the forest bare;
and in his temple all say, "Glory!"
The LORD sits enthroned over the flood;
the LORD sits enthroned as king forever.
May the LORD give strength to his people!
May the LORD bless his people with peace!

SECOND SUNDAY AFTER EPIPHANY

1 Samuel 3:1-10 (11-20)　　　　　　　　Psalm 139:1-6, 13-18
1 Corinthians 6:12-20　　　　　　　　　　　John 1:43-51

• **CALL TO WORSHIP** (responsively)
God's face shines upon us in Christ.
Turn your face up to him in joy.
Jesus shows God's way in the earth.
Come to God on that path.
The Spirit is God's saving power among all nations.
Be uplifted by the inspiration of the Holy Spirit.

• **PRAYER OF CONFESSION**
Giving God, ~~Uniting God, Indwelling God,~~ we are forgetful of the price you have paid for us in the dying and rising of your Son, Jesus Christ. We sin against our own body and yours when we are not mindful that these bodies, individually and collectively are shrines for your Holy Spirit. Forgive us if we live t~~oo much for food and drink and sex~~, not disciplined by the Spirit. Save us from all deadly sins by the power that raised Jesus from the dead through your Spirit within us. Amen.

• **DECLARATION OF GOD'S FORGIVENESS**
Hear the Good News! God exercises his saving power among the nations.
Friends, believe the Good News! In Jesus Christ, we are forgiven.

• **EXHORTATION**
When you have heard the call of Jesus to discipleship, follow him, and spend the rest of your life with him.

• **PRAYER OF THE DAY**
Lamb of God, Teacher of disciples, tend us and teach us, that we may live always within sight of you in gentle tractability and learn the simple obedience that will win us a name as reliable followers in your way. Amen.

• **PRAYER OF THANKSGIVING**
In broad daylight and in dead of night, in a communal sanctuary and in a quiet mind, you speak our name, God of the covenant, calling us to be your servants. We are honored to serve you and to join with all people who praise you. You have blessed us with all the good things of the earth and granted us the supreme gift of your Spirit to live in us. We would honor you

more fully in our bodies, living chastely, devoting our energies to serve you and others, lifting our voices to praise you, shouting in triumph as your justice guides nations. May all people praise you at last, O God, Creator, Judge, Savior/Lord, Holy Spirit. Amen.

• PRAYER OF DEDICATION
No gift of ours can match the gift of your Spirit, but without our bodies made available and obedient to the Spirit the church cannot be the body of Christ to do your work in the world. Use us and ours as we respond to your call in the gospel of Jesus Christ. Amen.

• PSALM 139:1-6, 13-18
O LORD, you have searched me and known me.
you discern my thoughts from far away.
You search out my path and my lying down,
and are acquainted with all my ways.
Even before a word is on my tongue,
O LORD, you know it completely.
You hem me in, behind and before,
and lay your hand upon me.
Such knowledge is too wonderful for me;
it is so high that I cannot attain it.
For it was you who formed my inward parts;
you knit me together in my mother's womb.
I praise you, for I am fearfully and wonderfully made.
Wonderful are your works; that I know very well.
My frame was not hidden from you,
when I was being made in secret,
intricately woven in the depths of the earth.
Your eyes beheld my unformed substance.
In your book were written all the days that were formed for me,
when none of them as yet existed.
How weighty to me are your thoughts, O God!
How vast is the sum of them!
I try to count them — they are more than the sand;
I come to the end — I am still with you.

THIRD SUNDAY AFTER EPIPHANY

Jonah 3:1-5, 10   Psalm 62:5-12
1 Corinthians 7:29-31   Mark 1:14-20

- **CALL TO WORSHIP**
Let your heart wait silently before God; our hope of salvation is in the ETERNAL.

- **PRAYER OF CONFESSION**
God of all times and places, ~~God in Israel and Nazareth~~*, God in our time and place, the meaning of time frequently escapes us. Grief and depression seem like forever. Joy and genuine communion seem so fleeting. Unpleasant duties are postponed; fancied pleasantries are prolonged. Dying takes others away, but we have difficulty facing our own mortality, and evaluating the significance of our own existence. Forgive our disregard for what you intend for us to do and be, for the sake of your temporal and eternal child, Jesus Christ. Amen.*

- **DECLARATION OF GOD'S FORGIVENESS**
Hear the Good News! The time has come; the kingdom of God is upon you; repent and believe the Gospel. Friends, believe the Good News. In Jesus Christ, we are forgiven.

- **EXHORTATION**
Hear the call of Jesus and in following him become a person, who in living with and for others, is fulfilled in time and eternity.

- **PRAYER OF THE DAY**
Master of all occupations, call us from pointless work to purposeful service in your community that we may be fully engaged with the Spirit in spreading God's Good News, by words and deeds. Amen.

- **PRAYER OF THANKSGIVING**
Just God, Loving Lord, Powerful Spirit, we rejoice with all who believe and obey your word on first hearing. We recover our gladness with all who having heard the word a second time, turn back to do what they were reluctant to do at first hearing. As faithless and frivolous as we may be, you show great patience with us, calling us to discipleship through your Son and our Lord Jesus Christ. How pointed you are about what is not good for us all! How loving is your teaching, living Word! How

sive is your Spirit's dealing with us! We respect your justice. We
¹ to your love. We are moved by your Spirit. We praise you, O God.
Amen.

• **PRAYER OF DEDICATION**
Timeless God, since the time we live in will not last long, we would invest both our time and our wealth in the work of your church which will not pass away. Increase our effectiveness in this company that our cooperative efforts may multiply our individual endeavors, to the glory of your name. Amen.

• **PSALM 62:5-12**
For God alone my soul waits in silence,
for my hope is from him.
He alone is my rock and my salvation, my fortress;
I shall not be shaken.
On God rests my deliverance and my honor;
my mighty rock, my refuge is in God.
Trust in him at all times, O people;
pour out your heart before him; God is a refuge for us.
Those of low estate are but a breath,
those of high estate are a delusion;
in the balances they go up;
they are together lighter than a breath.
Put no confidence in extortion,
and set no vain hopes on robbery;
if riches increase,
do not set your heart on them.
Once God has spoken;
twice have I heard this:
that power belongs to God,
and steadfast love belongs to you, O Lord.
For you repay to all according to their work.

FOURTH SUNDAY AFTER EPIPHANY

Deuteronomy 18:15-20 Psalm 111
1 Corinthians 8:1-13 Mark 1:21-28

- **CALL TO WORSHIP**
Happy is the person who takes delight in the word of the Lord and meditates upon it yielding the fruits of the Spirit in season.

- **PRAYER OF CONFESSION**
One God, undivided in being, undiverted in purpose, we confess that we are often distracted from waiting on you. Whether married or single, we are easily attracted and engrossed by worldly things. When married or responsible for a family, we may have additional cares that divide our minds, giving undue weight to the provision of daily bread and too little attention to what is good, what is seemly, what is true devotion to your work. Forgive faithless anxiety and half-hearted discipleship, unlike your exemplary Son, Jesus Christ, who was and is dedicated to you in body and in spirit. Amen.

- **DECLARATION OF GOD'S FORGIVENESS**
Hear the Good News! Jesus has power to rid us of unclean spirits, to cast out our sins. Friends, believe the Good News. In Jesus Christ, we are forgiven.

- **EXHORTATION**
Be free from anxious care and use your freedom to wait upon the Lord without distraction.

- **PRAYER OF THE DAY**
Jesus of Nazareth, Holy One of God, grant that we may hear the ring of authority in your teaching so that we may be rid of anything that profanes and shackles the human spirit, and be free to serve at your pleasure. Amen.

- **PRAYER OF THANKSGIVING**
God of purifying fire, God of true prophets, God of cleansing Spirit, of all the prophets you have sent speaking your word, no one measures up to the true authority of your Son, Jesus Christ. Of all the healers of body, mind, and spirit, none have touched the lives of the sick, the troubled, and the sinful, with as gentle power as Jesus of Nazareth. Of all the scholars and teachers we have known, none have influenced for good as many by their lives and teaching as the Spirit of your Holy Child, Jesus. We are dazzled

by visions of your holiness. We are astounded by the deepest revelations of your authority. We are sanctified by the inner baptism of your Spirit. You are worthy of all praise, O God. Amen.

• **PRAYER OF DEDICATION**
Lord of the church, we would serve you without distraction, taking the time, and giving the money that is needed, to give genuine expression to the care we have for your business. May it always be our aim to please you, Lord. Amen.

• **PSALM 111**
Praise the LORD!
I will give thanks to the LORD with my whole heart,
in the company of the upright,
in the congregation.
Great are the works of the LORD,
studied by all who delight in them.
Full of honor and majesty is his work,
and his righteousness endures forever.
He has gained renown by his wonderful deeds;
the LORD is gracious and merciful.
He provides food for those who fear him;
he is ever mindful of his covenant.
He has shown his people the power of his works,
in giving them the heritage of the nations.
The works of his hands are faithful and just;
all his precepts are trustworthy.
They are established forever and ever,
to be performed with faithfulness and uprightness.
He sent redemption to his people;
he has commanded his covenant forever.
Holy and awesome is his name.
The fear of the LORD is the beginning of wisdom;
all those who practice it have a good understanding.
His praise endures forever.

FIFTH SUNDAY AFTER EPIPHANY

Isaiah 40:21-31 Psalm 147:1-11, 20c
1 Corinthians 9:16-23 Mark 1:29-39

• **CALL TO WORSHIP**
O praise the Lord. How good it is to sing psalms to our God! How pleasant to praise him!

• **PRAYER OF CONFESSION**
God unlimited, God self-limited, God extending our limits, surely you do not expect us to accept suffering without complaint! We are frustrated with illnesses that rage on, keeping us from doing the things that bring us satisfaction and recognition. Long nights and months of futility seem such a waste to us. Too often we question why it should happen to us, thinking ourselves to be better than others. We forget the exposure of your Son Jesus, to all the circumstances of our mortality. We ignore the spiritual growth that could be ours to prepare us to minister to other sufferers. Forgive our resistance to the healing of spirit and body that your Spirit can enable through our faith in Jesus Christ. Amen.

• **DECLARATION OF GOD'S FORGIVENESS**
Hear the Good News! In the Spirit Jesus still comes healing those who suffer from various diseases and freeing many who are captives of evil. Friends, believe the Good News! In Jesus Christ, we are forgiven.

• **EXHORTATION**
Bear your part in spreading the Good News, whether in illness or health, weakness or strength, in the service of God.

• **PRAYER OF THE DAY**
Synagogue-preacher, sick-bed-visitor, exorcist-of-evil, so teach us, so heal us, so clear us of evil, that we may be ready learners and teachers, visitors of the sick and the shut-in, of other sinners, gathering around you in one needy company. Amen.

• **PRAYER OF THANKSGIVING**
Creator of stars, nurse to the wounded, healer of broken spirits: that you have power to rule the cosmos, fills us with awe. That you stoop to touch and heal us, fills us with amazement. You give new heart to the humble. We thank you for all that sustains life, human, vegetable, animal. Receive

the thanksgiving of all creation, the psalms of your people, the music of the birds, the sounds of all living things. Hear us wherever we gather to praise you name. Amen.

- **PRAYER OF DEDICATION**

God of the Gospel, we share the responsibility of spreading the Good News, with pastors and elders, evangelists and teachers, healers and nurses, identifying with all sorts and conditions of people in order to communicate the word of your grace in Jesus Christ. Amen.

- **PSALM 147:1-11, 20c**

Praise the LORD! How good it is to sing praises to our God;
for he is gracious, and a song of praise is fitting.
The LORD builds up Jerusalem;
he gathers the outcasts of Israel.
He heals the brokenhearted,
and binds up their wounds.
He determines the number of the stars;
he gives to all of them their names.
Great is our Lord, and abundant in power;
his understanding is beyond measure.
The LORD lifts up the downtrodden;
he casts the wicked to the ground.
Sing to the LORD with thanksgiving;
make melody to our God on the lyre.
He covers the heavens with clouds,
prepares rain for the earth, makes grass grow on the hills.
He gives to the animals their food,
and to the young ravens when they cry.
His delight is not in the strength of the horse,
nor his pleasure in the speed of a runner;
but the LORD takes pleasure in those who fear him,
in those who hope in his steadfast love.
Praise the LORD!

SIXTH SUNDAY AFTER EPIPHANY

2 Kings 5:1-14   Psalm 30
1 Corinthians 9:24-27   Mark 1:40-45

• CALL TO WORSHIP
Rejoice and be glad, good people, sing aloud before our Sovereign.

• PRAYER OF CONFESSION
God most high, God most humble, God most honest, forgive the pride that prevents us from repenting and being healed of our sins, the pride of place that will not let us appreciate the virtues of other places, the pride of race that scorns the accomplishments of other nationalities, the personal pride that will not respect the rights and privileges of others. We need the honesty to be humble with all and subservient to none but you after the example of Jesus Christ. Amen.

• DECLARATION OF GOD'S FORGIVENESS
Hear the Good News! As you have shown yourself willing to come to Christ, you will be forgiven and cleansed of all your sins. Friends, believe the Good News! In Jesus Christ, we are forgiven.

• EXHORTATION
Strive for spiritual excellence as an athlete trains and competes for less enduring laurels.

• PRAYER OF THE DAY
Healing and humble Christ, help us to serve the needs of others without concern for the attention and praise of the many, content to know that we have responded to the cry for help. Amen.

• PRAYER OF THANKSGIVING
Gracious God, guiltless Christ, gladdening Spirit, our joy is in knowing that you are forgiving and do not hold our sins against us forever. When we give up the attempted concealment of our guilt, you enfold us in your saving and loving arms, putting our sin and guilt behind us. We find refuge with you in times of distress that come as great floods threatening to sweep us away. We rejoice in your unfailing love. Amen.

• PRAYER OF DEDICATION
Generous God, though there is no way we can repay you for your kindness and mercy in Jesus Christ, receive our offerings as a token of gratitude and enable us to share the Good News with others through this community. Amen.

• PSALM 30

I will extol you, O LORD, for you have drawn me up,
and did not let my foes rejoice over me.
O LORD my God, I cried to you for help,
and you have healed me.
O LORD, you brought up my soul from Sheol,
restored me to life from among those gone down to the Pit.
Sing praises to the LORD, O you his faithful ones,
and give thanks to his holy name.
For his anger is but for a moment;
his favor is for a lifetime.
Weeping may linger for the night,
but joy comes with the morning.
As for me, I said in my prosperity, "I shall never be moved."
By your favor, O LORD, you had established me as a strong mountain;
you hid your face;
I was dismayed.
To you, O LORD, I cried,
and to the LORD I made supplication:
"What profit is there in my death, if I go down to the Pit?
Will the dust praise you? Will it tell of your faithfulness?
Hear, O LORD, and be gracious to me!
O LORD, be my helper!"
You have turned my mourning into dancing;
you have taken off my sackcloth and clothed me with joy,
so that my soul may praise you and not be silent.
O LORD my God, I will give thanks to you forever.

SEVENTH SUNDAY AFTER EPIPHANY

Isaiah 43:18-25   Psalm 41
2 Corinthians 1:18-22   Mark 2:1-12

• CALL TO WORSHIP
In Christ Jesus every one of God's promises is a "Yes." For this reason through him let us say the "Amen," to the glory of God.

• PRAYER OF CONFESSION
Patient Parent, holy and forgiving, we would rather speak to those who speak to us, to love those who love us in return. We enjoy the common enthusiasms of our own country and its people. We would rather hate our enemies than pray for them and for those who harass us. The passive resistance that Jesus teaches seems unworkable to us and unfair, giving the advantage to our adversaries, at the expense of our personal rights. Forgive us for following our own devices and not obeying the instruction of Jesus Christ. Amen.

• DECLARATION OF GOD'S FORGIVENESS
Hear the Good News! To us as to others, Jesus says, "Your sins are forgiven." Friends, believe the Good News! In Jesus Christ, we are forgiven.

• EXHORTATION
Do not bear hatred for your brothers and sisters in your heart. Do not take revenge or cherish grudges. The Lord says to love your neighbor as yourself.

• PRAYER OF THE DAY
Your goodness, O God, knows no bounds. Increase our goodness beyond its present limits to higher stages of maturity, that our love and forgiveness may become more nearly like that of your Son, our Savior, Jesus Christ. Amen.

• PRAYER OF THANKSGIVING
Gracious God, your benevolence is not limited to the deserving or those who would receive the many benefits that we take for granted. You make your sun to rise on good and bad alike and send the rain on the honest and the dishonest. We are grateful for all your gifts and for the friendships that have come to us without our seeking them, for those who have been kind and helpful to us without any initiative on our part. Help us to show our

thankfulness by taking the initiative in reaching out to others who need friends, by going the extra mile to be helpful, especially for those who may not be able to ask for help. We appreciate being part of your family gathered in the Spirit. We are humbled by the thought that as we belong to Christ, we belong to you, God of all. Amen.

- **PRAYER OF DEDICATION**

You honor us, Divine Spirit, by making your home within us. Make us more fitting temples for your habitation, urging us toward the maturity and open-heartedness that is the genius of our Divine Parent. Bless our church as a means to that end, through Jesus Christ our Lord. Amen.

- **PSALM 41**

Happy are those who consider the poor;
the LORD delivers them in the day of trouble.
The LORD protects them and keeps them alive;
they are called happy in the land.
You do not give them up to the will of their enemies.
The LORD sustains them on their sickbed;
in their illness you heal all their infirmities.
As for me, I said, "O LORD, be gracious to me;
heal me, for I have sinned against you."
My enemies wonder in malice when I will die,
and my name perish.
And when they come to see me, they utter empty words,
while their hearts gather mischief;
when they go out, they tell it abroad.
All who hate me whisper together about me;
they imagine the worst for me.
They think that a deadly thing has fastened on me,
that I will not rise again from where I lie.
Even my bosom friend in whom I trusted,
who ate of my bread, has lifted the heel against me.
But you, O LORD, be gracious to me,
and raise me up, that I may repay them.
By this I know that you are pleased with me;
because my enemy has not triumphed over me.
But you have upheld me because of my integrity,
and set me in your presence forever.
Blessed be the LORD, the God of Israel,
from everlasting to everlasting.
Amen
and Amen.

EIGHTH SUNDAY AFTER EPIPHANY

Hosea 2:14-20　　　　　　　　　　　　　　Psalm 103:1-13, 22
2 Corinthians 3:1-6　　　　　　　　　　　　　　　Mark 2:18-22

• CALL TO WORSHIP
Bless God from your innermost heart and hallow God's name, forgetting none of the benefits of divine pardon and healing.

• PRAYER OF CONFESSION
Liberating God, loving Christ, loyal Spirit, like Israel we can forget our liberation from bondage, and ignore the covenant you have made with us in the new testament. We confess our infidelity to the loving expectations you have of us as a community called out of service to lesser things to your worship and your mission in the world. We have forgotten the pledges of love that we have made and are unworthy of your unfailing devotion. Forgive us for the sake of our Savior, Jesus Christ. Amen.

• DECLARATION OF GOD'S FORGIVENESS
Hear the Good News! God pardons all our guilt, not treating us as our sins deserve or requiting us for our misdeeds. Friends, believe the Good News! In Jesus Christ, we are forgiven.

• EXHORTATION
Put your reliance on God through Christ and depend only on the qualifications the Spirit gives. None of us in ourselves can serve God worthily.

• PRAYER OF THE DAY
Leader and Teacher with all authority, speak to us as to the first disciples that we may leave behind all lesser callings for the privilege of living with you in daily communion and the service of others in whatever vocation. Amen.

• PRAYER OF THANKSGIVING
God of all times, contemporary Christ, living Spirit, we give thanks to you for all in whose lives we have read the writing of your hand. Our hearts have been warmed by the glow of the Spirit's fire. We have seen with wonder and joy the changes you have made in the lives of people, even our own lives. We are grateful that the condemning law gives way to the life-giving Spirit. Alleluia. Amen.

• PRAYER OF DEDICATION
Receive our donations and our discipleship, eternal Christ, that our daily work and our daily witness may call others to your service. Amen.

SALM 103:1-13
ess the LORD, O my soul,
and all that is within me, bless his holy name.
Bless the LORD, O my soul, and do not forget all his benefits —
who forgives all your iniquity, who heals all your diseases,
who redeems your life from the Pit,
who crowns you with steadfast love and mercy,
who satisfies you with good as long as you live
so that your youth is renewed like the eagle's.
The LORD works vindication
and justice for all who are oppressed.
He made known his ways to Moses,
his acts to the people of Israel.
The LORD is merciful and gracious,
slow to anger and abounding in steadfast love.
He will not always accuse,
nor will he keep his anger forever.
He does not deal with us according to our sins,
nor repay us according to our iniquities.
For as the heavens are high above the earth,
so great is his steadfast love toward those who fear him;
as far as the east is from the west,
so far he removes our transgressions from us.
As a father has compassion for his children,
so the LORD has compassion for those who fear him.
For he knows how we were made;
he remembers that we are dust.
As for mortals, their days are like grass;
they flourish like a flower of the field;
for the wind passes over it, and it is gone, and its place knows it no more.
But the steadfast love of the LORD is from everlasting to
everlasting on those who fear him,
and his righteousness to children's children,
to those who keep his covenant and remember to do his commandments.
The LORD has established his throne in the heavens,
and his kingdom rules over all.
Bless the LORD, O you his angels,
you mighty ones who do his bidding, obedient to his spoken word.
Bless the LORD, all his hosts, his ministers that do his will.
Bless the LORD, all his works,
in all places of his dominion. Bless the LORD, O my soul.

NINTH SUNDAY AFTER EPIPHANY

Deuteronomy 5:12-15   Psalm 81:1-10
2 Corinthians 4:5-12   Mark 2:23-3:6

• CALL TO WORSHIP
Worship the God who said, "Let light shine out of darkness," who has shone in our hearts to give the light of the knowledge of the glory of God in the face of Jesus Christ.

• PRAYER OF CONFESSION
Gracious God, Compassionate Christ, Generous Spirit, what a treasure you have given us in the church. Save us from unwarranted pride and dogmatism that obscure our fallibility and put in the shadow the truth and grace that belong only to you. Grant us modesty and true humility in the sharing of our convictions and discrimination as to their source. Let your light continue to shine on us that we may be saved; through Jesus Christ our Lord. Amen.

• DECLARATION OF GOD'S FORGIVENESS
Hear the Good News! The light of the knowledge of the glory of God has shone upon us in the face of Jesus Christ. Friends, believe the Good News! In Jesus Christ, we are forgiven.

• EXHORTATION
May the life of Jesus also be made visible in our bodies.

• PRAYER OF THE DAY
Lord of Time, teach us how to use our time wisely in labor and rest with concern for others' healing and health as well as our own. Amen.

• PRAYER OF THANKSGIVING
Creator of all things, Firstborn of all Creation, Timeless Spirit: how wonderful are the cycles of your universe and the measures of time that govern our life in days and weeks and years. What suspense spices our days in the uncertainties of climate that provoke adaptability in us and all your creatures! What delight we may take in good weather after what we call bad weather. Give us wisdom to enjoy also the changing moods of our spirits, always giving thanks to you in good times and in bad; through Jesus Christ your Son, who shared our human condition in all its variation except sin. Amen.

- **PRAYER OF DEDICATION**

God of Eternity, of time, of history, receive our offerings as a measure of our devotion to you in hours and days and years; through Jesus Christ our Lord. Amen.

- **PSALM 80:1-10**

Give ear, O Shepherd of Israel,
you who lead Joseph like a flock!
You who are enthroned upon the cherubim,
shine forth before Ephraim and Benjamin and Manasseh.
Stir up your might,
and come to save us!
Restore us, O God;
let your face shine, that we may be saved.
O LORD God of hosts, how long will you be angry
with your people's prayers?
You have fed them with the bread of tears,
and given them tears to drink in full measure.
You make us the scorn of our neighbors;
our enemies laugh among themselves.
Restore us, O God of hosts;
let your face shine, that we may be saved.
You brought a vine out of Egypt;
you drove out the nations and planted it.
You cleared the ground for it;
it took deep root and filled the land.
The mountains were covered with its shade,
the mighty cedars with its branches.

LAST SUNDAY AFTER EPIPHANY
(Transfiguration)

2 Kings 2:1-12　　　　　　　　　　　　　　　Psalm 50:1-6
2 Corinthians 4:3-6　　　　　　　　　　　　　　Mark 9:2-9

• CALL TO WORSHIP
Gather to Christ, Christians, for he has given himself to make a new covenant with all of us. His self-sacrifice has established the new testament which includes all believers.

• PRAYER OF CONFESSION
God of the gospel, Christ of God, Spirit of God, forgive us if we become enamoured of others, great as they are, and do not center our lives and our loyalties on the One who is your beloved son. Excuse our enthusiasms for lesser luminaries, the gods of our passing age, whose fascination and fame may distract us from following Jesus Christ with undivided devotion. Amen.

• DECLARATION OF GOD'S FORGIVENESS
Hear the good news! The gospel of the glory of Christ, who is the very image of God, has dawned upon us so that we can avoid the way to perdition. Friends, believe the good news! In Jesus Christ, we are forgiven.

• EXHORTATION
Proclaim not yourselves nor any institution instead of Jesus Christ as Lord and ourselves his servants.

• PRAYER OF THE DAY
Transfiguring Spirit, clear our sight of all unbelief so that seeing Christ in all his divine perfection we may worship him exclusively and look for no other leader into the realm of God. Amen.

• PRAYER OF THANKSGIVING
Speaking God, shining God, judging God, we celebrate the beauty and order of the world which you have summoned into being. We respect the justice that you proclaim in the orderliness of the heavens and that you seek to restore among us in the revelation of your glory in the face of Jesus Christ. We give thanks for all who have passed along the heritage of faith and the call to serve you. We will hallow your name for ever and no other. Amen.

- **PRAYER OF DEDICATION**

Infinite God, your presence is confined by no shelter, nor can all nature radiate your glory. Reveal your gracious glory again in the face of Jesus Christ and in the works of his body the church. Amen.

- **PSALM 50:1-6**

The mighty one, God the LORD, speaks
and summons the earth from the rising of the sun to its setting.
Out of Zion, the perfection of beauty, God shines forth.
Our God comes and does not keep silence,
before him is a devouring fire,
and a mighty tempest all around him.
He calls to the heavens above and to the earth,
that he may judge his people:
"Gather to me my faithful ones,
who made a covenant with me by sacrifice!"
The heavens declare his righteousness,
for God himself is judge.

ASH WEDNESDAY

Joel 2:1-2, 12-17a or Isaiah 58:1-12 Psalm 51:1-17
2 Corinthians 5:20b-6:10 Matthew 6:1-6, 16-21

• CALL TO WORSHIP
Take joy in your salvation and be willing to obey God as the Spirit prompts you.

• PRAYER OF CONFESSION
God above all, you have created us from the ground up and in Christ came to our turf, to show us again that the earth is yours and you have made all things to be good. Your own Spirit infused life into the lifeless so that the human race should be distinct not in its physical properties but in its ability to control behavior individually and socially. Forgive our lack of self-control and our abuse of what you have created for the good of all. May such fasting and penitence as we may practice enable us to balance things out and to bring the spiritual and the physical into equilibrium, following the example of Jesus Christ. Amen.

• DECLARATION OF GOD'S FORGIVENESS
Hear the Good News! God appointed the sinless Christ to share our sin in order that in union with him we might share the goodness of God. Friends, believe the Good News. In Jesus Christ, we are forgiven.

• EXHORTATION
Having received God's grace in Christ, do not let it be wasted, but express it to others enriching them as well.

• PRAYER OF THE DAY
Distinguished and distinguishing Spirit, grant us wisdom, so that both our fasting and our charitable actions are inconspicuous, Then only you will know what we have done and we will be content with your private reward. Amen.

• PRAYER OF THANKSGIVING
Maker, Sharer, and Shaper of the human Spirit, we are thankful that we have not been cast in stone that can not be reshaped. You forgive our failures and give us further opportunities to restore some of the beauty of your image. We can be thankful even for the trouble and suffering that brings us closer to you in prayer. Then at least we may recognize our need to depend on you. We welcome this Lenten season as a time of personal renewal. Amen.

• **PRAYER OF DEDICATION**
Eternal God, Ruler of time and space, we offer to you an expanded portion of our time and increased concentration of our attention during this Lenten season for our own growth in grace and in love for your family. Amen.

• **PSALM 51:1-17**
Have mercy on me, O God, according to your steadfast love;
according to your abundant mercy blot out my transgressions.
Wash me thoroughly from my iniquity,
and cleanse me from my sin.
For I know my transgressions,
and my sin is ever before me.
Against you, you alone, have I sinned,
and done what is evil in your sight,
so that you are justified in your sentence
and blameless when you pass judgment.
Indeed, I was born guilty,
a sinner when my mother conceived me.
You desire truth in the inward being;
therefore teach me wisdom in my secret heart.
Purge me with hyssop, and I shall be clean;
wash me, and I shall be whiter than snow.
Let me hear joy and gladness;
let the bones that you have crushed rejoice.
Hide your face from my sins,
and blot out all my iniquities.
Create in me a clean heart, O God,
and put a new and right spirit within me.
Do not cast me away from your presence,
and do not take your holy spirit from me.
Restore to me the joy of your salvation,
and sustain in me a willing spirit.

FIRST SUNDAY IN LENT

Genesis 9:8-17　　　　　　　　　　　　　　　　Psalm 25:1-10
1 Peter 3:18-22　　　　　　　　　　　　　　　　Mark 1:9-15

• **CALL TO WORSHIP**
Look for signs of the covenant which God makes with us and our children to endless generations. No one who hopes in God will be put to shame.

• **PRAYER OF CONFESSION**
Savior-God, at whose right hand sits the Risen Christ, having received the submission of angels; without our baptism we could not come before you in good conscience. Without the death of Christ for our sins, we would be condemned. We are among the unjust for whom the just Christ willingly suffered. Our only hope of salvation is in the resurrection of Jesus Christ, who was put to death in the body and brought to life in the spirit. Were it not for that Good News we too would be imprisoned by our sin and guilt. Grant us continuing repentance and faith in the gospel; under the rainbow of your covenant and our baptism in the name of the Father, and of the Son, and of the Holy Spirit. Amen.

• **DECLARATION OF GOD'S FORGIVENESS**
Hear the Good News! Christ died for our sins once and for all. He, the just, suffered for the unjust to bring us to God. Friends, believe the Good News! In Jesus Christ, we are forgiven.

• **EXHORTATION**
Through these forty days and all the days of your life, resist the temptations of God's adversaries, in the strength that God is willing to give you.

• **PRAYER OF THE DAY**
God of imprisoned prophets, so rule in our hearts that we may turn back from every evil way and, believing the Gospel, be sent by the spirit to people and places where the Good News has yet to come; in the name of Jesus Christ. Amen.

• **PRAYER OF THANKSGIVING**
Creator of All Life, Person from whom comes all persons, Maker of Covenants, we see in the rainbow your promise never to destroy all life by flood. We find in the church an ark to save us from spiritual death. We give thanks to you for the continuing sign of baptism to remind us of the death and resurrection of Jesus Christ, the just for the unjust to bring us to you.

We rejoice that he is at your right hand, being raised to high honor, after receiving the submission of angelic authorities and powers. May all living things praise you. May all persons worship and obey you. May all parties who covenant with you keep their faith, or renew their promises, through Jesus Christ our Lord. Amen.

• PRAYER OF DEDICATION
Holy God, we are unworthy to stand before you except by the grace of our baptism. Sanctify our gifts by the spirit that they may be worthy of your use in the proclamation of the Good News of Jesus Christ. Amen.

• PSALM 25:1-10
To you, O LORD, I lift up my soul.
O my God, in you I trust;
do not let me be put to shame;
do not let my enemies exult over me.
Do not let those who wait for you be put to shame;
let them be ashamed who are wantonly treacherous.
Make me to know your ways, O LORD;
teach me your paths.
Lead me in your truth, and teach me,
for you are the God of my salvation;
for you I wait all day long.
Be mindful of your mercy, O LORD,
and of your steadfast love, for they have been from of old.
Do not remember the sins of my youth or my transgressions;
according to your steadfast love remember me, for your goodness' sake, O LORD!
Good and upright is the LORD;
therefore he instructs sinners in the way.
He leads the humble in what is right,
and teaches the humble his way.
All the paths of the LORD are steadfast love and faithfulness,
for those who keep his covenant and his decrees.

SECOND SUNDAY IN LENT

Genesis 17:1-7, 15-16　　　　　　　　　　Psalm 22:23-31
Romans 4:13-25　　　　　　　　　　Mark 8:31-38 or 9:2-9

• **CALL TO WORSHIP**
Let all who see God be joyful in heart and exult in the hallowed name. Live in the divine presence always as a source of your strength.

• **PRAYER OF CONFESSION**
Divine Thinker, Messianic Sufferer, Loving Spirit, we confess that we long for glory but avoid suffering. To be recognized and praised pleases us, but we turn back from the cross of unpleasant truth-telling and the defense of unpopular causes. Forgive our unwillingness to follow Christ in carrying our own crosses and living the truth as your Spirit would do if we willingly submitted to such guidance. Pardon pride and the sinful advice that we give others who are prepared to be humble like Jesus, in whose name we pray. Amen.

• **DECLARATION OF GOD'S FORGIVENESS**
Hear the Good News! Like Abraham's faith in God, our faith can be counted for the good, because Jesus was given up to death for our misdeeds and raised from the dead to justify us in the sight of God. Friends, believe the Good News. In Jesus Christ, we are forgiven.

• **EXHORTATION**
Hear the call of Jesus to be a disciple. Bear your cross bravely and risk your life that in the end you may be saved.

• **PRAYER OF THE DAY**
Christ of Cross and Crown, strengthen us in unselfishness and in faith that in this wicked and godless age, we may be faithful disciples in both word and deed and thus honor your name and the name given us in our baptism. Amen.

• **PRAYER OF THANKSGIVING**
God of patriarch and matriarch, of disciple and unbeliever, we are thankful for the call of Jesus to believe in him and to share in the acceptance you grant to all who believe in him. We would thank you by our actions as well as our adoration, by our service as well as our prayers, our offerings as well as our promises. What noble but human ancestors

in the faith you have given us to set an example of what can be done by you when your people are willing. We praise your grace and give glory to your name. Amen.

• PRAYER OF DEDICATION
Matchless Giver, receive our offerings of ourselves and our possessions, insignificant beside the gift of Christ, but precious to you as signs of our obedient cross-bearing hallowed by the Spirit. Amen.

• PSALM 22:23-31
You who fear the LORD, praise him!
All you offspring of Jacob, glorify him;
stand in awe of him, all you offspring of Israel!
For he did not despise or abhor the affliction of the afflicted;
he did not hide his face from me, but heard when I cried to him.
From you comes my praise in the great congregation;
my vows I will pay before those who fear him.
The poor shall eat and be satisfied;
those who seek him shall praise the LORD.
May your hearts live forever!
All the ends of the earth shall remember and turn to the LORD;
and all the families of the nations shall worship before him.
For dominion belongs to the LORD,
and he rules over the nations.
To him, indeed, shall all who sleep in the earth bow down;
before him shall bow all who go down to the dust,
and I shall live for him.
Posterity will serve him;
future generations will be told about the Lord,
and proclaim his deliverance to a people yet unborn,
saying that he has done it.

THIRD SUNDAY IN LENT

Exodus 20:1-17　　　　　　　　　　　　　　Psalm 19:1-14
1 Corinthians 1:18-25　　　　　　　　　　　John 2:13-22

• CALL TO WORSHIP
God calls us to faith in the Christ nailed to the cross, as wisdom wiser than ours and power stronger than ours. Hear that call.

• PRAYER OF CONFESSION
God of the law, Christ of the cross, Spirit of purity, we confess that we have broken your commandments, commercialized your church, compromised the simplicity of the faith. We are too ready to choose our favorite commandments and to ignore the others to minimize our guilt. We excuse our breaking of some of them by pointing out that we are keeping the others. Forgive any self-righteousness that ignores the need for the sacrifice of Christ for our sins and the cleansing of the Spirit for our holiness. Amen.

• DECLARATION OF GOD'S FORGIVENESS
Hear the Good News! God is not only lawgiver but redeemer and will cleanse us from the secret sins that have escaped our own attention. Friends, believe the Good News! In Jesus Christ, we are forgiven.

• EXHORTATION
Be enlightened by all that God commands. Your spirit will be revived by God's law and you will find reward in the keeping of the commandments.

• PRAYER OF THE DAY
Let our zeal for your house, Lord Jesus, be exceeded only by our desire to be pure in heart and thus enabled to see you in your ultimate glory. Amen.

• PRAYER OF THANKSGIVING
God of wisdom, we praise your name. Christ of the cross, we give thanks for your loving and forgiving death for our sins. Purifying Spirit, we celebrate the liberation from our guilt as you renew and revive our spirits. We are humbled by the dignity to which you call us despite our faults and failing. Thanks be to you, O God. Amen.

• PRAYER OF DEDICATION
Your house, O God, is meant to be a house of prayer. May nothing we do here be inappropriate to that purpose but be supportive of your purposes in Jesus Christ. Amen.

• PSALM 19:1-14

The heavens are telling the glory of God;
and the firmament proclaims his handiwork.
Day to day pours forth speech,
and night to night declares knowledge.
There is no speech, nor are there words;
their voice is not heard;
yet their voice goes out through all the earth,
and their words to the end of the world.
In the heavens he has set a tent for the sun,
which comes out like a bridegroom from his wedding canopy,
and like a strong man runs its course with joy.
Its rising is from the end of the heavens,
and its circuit to the end of them;
and nothing is hid from its heat.
The law of the LORD is perfect, reviving the soul;
the decrees of the LORD are sure, making wise the simple;
the precepts of the LORD are right, rejoicing the heart;
the commandment of the LORD is clear, enlightening the eyes;
the fear of the LORD is pure, enduring forever;
the ordinances of the LORD are true and righteous altogether.
More to be desired are they than gold, even much fine gold;
sweeter also than honey, and drippings of the honeycomb.
Moreover by them is your servant warned;
in keeping them there is great reward.
But who can detect their errors?
Clear me from hidden faults.
Keep back your servant also from the insolent;
do not let them have dominion over me.
Then I shall be blameless,
and innocent of great transgression.
Let the words of my mouth and the meditation of my heart be
acceptable to you, O LORD, my rock and my redeemer.

FOURTH SUNDAY IN LENT

Numbers 21:4-9　　　　　　　　　Psalm 107:1-3, 17-22
Ephesians 2:1-10　　　　　　　　　　　　John 3:14-21

- **CALL TO WORSHIP**

Do not avoid the light of God but expose yourself to it. Come to the light so that it will be clear that God is involved in all the good things that you do.

- **PRAYER OF CONFESSION**

Ruler of our enemies and our allies, adversary of evil everywhere, Savior of all who put their trust in you, we confess that we do not always turn your light on ourselves as carefully as on the behavior of others. We are too prone to spotlight the failures and injustices of other societies than our own. In our private lives we have been subject to the whims of our sensual natures convinced that the natural is always good, ignoring your prohibitions against what is hurtful to both others and ourselves. Forgive our incomplete obedience to your prompting and save us from our sins by your grace in Jesus Christ. Amen.

- **DECLARATION OF GOD'S FORGIVENESS**

Hear the Good News! God is rich in mercy, for the great love he bore us, brought us to life with Christ even when we were dead in our sins; it is by his grace that you are saved. Friends, believe the Good News! In Jesus Christ, we are forgiven.

- **EXHORTATION**

Devote yourselves to the good deeds for which God has designed you.

- **PRAYER OF THE DAY**

Divine descendant from heaven, human ascendant from earth, let the light of love from your cross continue to shine in our world so that all who look to you in faith may live, no longer under judgment, but in grateful allegiance to you. Amen.

- **PRAYER OF THANKSGIVING**

Gracious Sovereign, we praise the mercy that you have shown to your rebel subjects who have returned to live under your loving rule. Divine treasurer, we are thankful for all the resources of your grace that enrich our lives. Divine designer, we celebrate the handiworks you have created, retooling us to accomplish the purpose of your realm. You have brought us out of death into life, out of subservience to evil, into the freedom of all that is godly and good. How great is your kindness to us in Jesus Christ. Amen.

- **PRAYER OF DEDICATION**
No sanctuary is worthy of you, O God, but we bring our offerings not only to furnish this house of prayer, but to manifest to the world the gift of salvation that you freely offer in Jesus Christ. Amen.

- **PSALM 107:1-3, 17-22**
O give thanks to the LORD, for he is good;
for his steadfast love endures forever.
Let the redeemed of the LORD say so,
those he redeemed from trouble
and gathered in from the lands,
from the east and from the west,
from the north and from the south.
Some were sick through their sinful ways,
and because of their iniquities endured affliction;
they loathed any kind of food,
and they drew near to the gates of death.
Then they cried to the LORD in their trouble,
and he saved them from their distress;
he sent out his word and healed them,
and delivered them from destruction.
Let them thank the LORD for his steadfast love,
for his wonderful works to humankind.
And let them offer thanksgiving sacrifices,
and tell of his deeds with songs of joy.

FIFTH SUNDAY IN LENT

Jeremiah 31:31-34 Psalm 51:1-12 or 119:9-16
Hebrews 5:5-10 John 12:20-33

• **CALL TO WORSHIP**
Come to see Jesus, even though his glory is a cross and to follow him may mean a cross of your own.

• **PRAYER OF CONFESSION**
Renewer of covenants, divine-human Pledge of the new covenant, Spirit of the covenant, forgive our wrongdoing and remember our sins against us no more. Though you are known by the high and the lowly, yet we have not reached the time when it will not be necessary to teach one another to know you. Or is it that knowing you we decline to obey you? As you were patient with Israel and Judah when they broke your covenant, we implore your patience with us, who are the children of the new covenant, made with the world in the cross of Jesus Christ, your Son. Much of what we know has not yet been incorporated into our lives and we need a willing Spirit, new and steadfast like your obedient child, Jesus. Amen.

• **DECLARATION OF GOD'S FORGIVENESS**
Hear the Good News! God has named as our high priest, the Son who learned obedience and was made perfect in suffering, thus becoming the source of eternal salvation to all who obey him. Friends, believe the Good News! In Jesus Christ, we are forgiven.

• **EXHORTATION**
Follow the Son of Man, that where Christ is, there you may serve and in serving be honored by our Divine Parent.

• **PRAYER OF THE DAY**
Christ of the cross, drive out the prince of this world from strongholds in and around us, that being freed from the hold of evil we may be drawn to you and glorify your name and the name of the One who sent you. Amen.

• **PRAYER OF THANKSGIVING**
God of justice, delivering champion, purifying Spirit, you give us joy in remembering our deliverance from the power of the evil one through the victory of Christ and the cross. You have not driven us from you, but created pure hearts within us that we might remain near you. We will sing the praise of your justice and commit ourselves to teach the way that leads

to you, to other transgressors, who may also turn to you again and know the joy of your salvation. Receive our praise, God of old and new covenants, through Christ our high priest and by the Holy Spirit. Amen.

• **PRAYER OF DEDICATION**
We would be your people, O God, as you have offered to be our God. Through your church, lift up your Son, Jesus as a continuing high priest interceding for all sinners, to the glory of your name. Amen.

• **PSALM 51:1-12**
Have mercy on me, O God, according to your steadfast love;
according to your abundant mercy blot out my transgressions.
Wash me thoroughly from my iniquity,
and cleanse me from my sin.
For I know my transgressions,
and my sin is ever before me.
Against you, you alone, have I sinned,
and done what is evil in your sight,
so that you are justified in your sentence
and blameless when you pass judgment.
Indeed, I was born guilty,
a sinner when my mother conceived me.
You desire truth in the inward being;
therefore teach me wisdom in my secret heart.
Purge me with hyssop, and I shall be clean;
wash me, and I shall be whiter than snow.
Let me hear joy and gladness;
let the bones that you have crushed rejoice.
Hide your face from my sins,
and blot out all my iniquities.
Create in me a clean heart, O God,
and put a new and right spirit within me.
Do not cast me away from your presence,
and do not take your holy spirit from me.
Restore to me the joy of your salvation,
and sustain in me a willing spirit.

(or)

• PSALM 119:9-16
How can young people keep their way pure?
By guarding it according to your word.
With my whole heart I seek you;
do not let me stray from your commandments.
I treasure your word in my heart,
so that I may not sin against you.
Blessed are you, O LORD; teach me your statutes.
With my lips I declare all the ordinances of your mouth.
I delight in the way of your decrees
as much as in all riches.
I will meditate on your precepts,
and fix my eyes on your ways.
I will delight in your statutes;
I will not forget your word.

SIXTH SUNDAY IN LENT

+Liturgy of the Palms

Isaiah 50:4-9a   Psalm 118:1-2,19-29
Philippians 2:5-11   Mark 11:1-11 or John 12:12-16

+++Liturgy of the Passion

Isaiah 50:4-9a   Psalm 31:9-16
Philippians 2:5-11   Mark 14:1-15:47 or Mark 15:1-39, (40-47)

• +CALL TO WORSHIP
Blessed in the name of the Anointed One are all who come; we bless you from the house of Christ.

• +++CALL TO WORSHIP
If you saw him in the street, would you turn quickly away? Or would you welcome him, saying, "I put my trust in you. You are my God."

• +PRAYER OF CONFESSION
God of covenants, old and new, carved in stone and written in heart, we confess that we have broken our agreements with you as with others and need your forgiveness for our wrongdoing. Forget our sins and continue your patience to us. We avoid learning because it often entails suffering and to avoid suffering we seek the way of ease, forgetting that even Jesus learned by the things that he suffered. Forgive us, we pray in his saving name. Amen.

• +++PRAYER OF CONFESSION
All-seeing God, all-loving God, all-encompassing God, we confess that we can ignore what we see, that we can be indifferent to what is too painful to acknowledge, that we can push aside what intrudes on our personal comfort. Forgive such self-centeredness, our lack of compassion, our lack of involvement. Pardon our reluctant and partial imitation of the suffering servanthood of Jesus Christ. Amen.

• +DECLARATION OF GOD'S FORGIVENESS
Hear the Good News! Jesus is the source of eternal salvation for all who obey him. Friends, believe the Good News! In Jesus Christ, we are forgiven.

• +++ DECLARATION OF GOD'S FORGIVENESS
Hear the Good News! The curtain of the temple was torn in two from top to bottom signifying our ready access to the mercy seat of God. Friends, believe the Good News! In Jesus Christ, we are forgiven.

- **+EXHORTATION**
Learn obedience and gain maturity by humble submission in prayer to the will of God.

- **+++EXHORTATION**
Be humble in your attitude toward one another and in that way show that your life is like that of our humble Savior, Christ Jesus.

- **+PRAYER OF THE DAY**
Patient Teacher, when we are stubborn as mules, show us a docile donkey, so that when we are willing to bear the burden you place on us, we may find ourselves bearing the Christ. Amen.

- **+++PRAYER OF THE DAY**
Crucified One, we need your humble spirit if we are to face the ridicule of the unbelieving without retaliation and accept persecution with resignation. So empty us of pride and we will be more like you. Amen.

- **+PRAYER OF THANKSGIVING**
We praise you, O God, for the one who comes in your name. We hail the humble Sovereign who comes in the nobility of servanthood and suffering rather than in pomp and circumstance. We welcome the coming reign of the gentle giant who blesses children but conquers evil as our champion. Hallowed be the name of Jesus, your anointed One, and the One we choose to follow. Glory to God in the highest. Glory to God in the lowest. Glory to the Spirit who lives in us. Amen.

- **+++PRAYER OF THANKSGIVING**
What a stake you have struck into the earth, O God! What a gruesome but gracious tree you have planted on Calvary! How can we find the words to express our thanksgiving for the gush of life that flows from the death of your crucified Son? The hallowed symbol of the cross and the bread and cup of the table of the new covenant will be our sacrament to the end of time and the everlasting feast of eternity! Amen.

- **+PRAYER OF DEDICATION**
Eternal One, though our gifts may wither like palms, and our persons age and grow weak, yet receive what we give to you in money and in service, and accomplish what will survive with us in eternity. Amen.

- **+++PRAYER OF DEDICATION**
All the earnings of my lifetime, magnanimous God, are miniscule beside the offering of your Bethlehem Child and Calvary Son, so may I offer myself, my lifetime, my eternity in worship and servanthood. Amen.

- **+PSALM 118:1-2, 19-29**

O give thanks to the LORD, for he is good;
his steadfast love endures forever!
Let Israel say, "His steadfast love endures forever."
Open to me the gates of righteousness,
that I may enter through them and give thanks to the LORD.
This is the gate of the LORD;
the righteous shall enter through it.
I thank you that you have answered me
and have become my salvation.
The stone that the builders rejected
has become the chief cornerstone.
This is the LORD's doing; it is marvelous in our eyes.
This is the day that the LORD has made; let us rejoice and be glad in it.
Save us, we beseech you, O LORD!
O LORD, we beseech you, give us success!
Blessed is the one who comes in the name of the LORD.
We bless you from the house of the LORD.
The LORD is God, and he has given us light.
Bind the festal procession with branches,
up to the horns of the altar.
You are my God, and I will give thanks to you;
you are my God, I will extol you.
O give thanks to the LORD, for he is good,
for his steadfast love endures forever.

- **+++PSALM 31:9-16**

Open to me the gates of righteousness,
that I may enter through them and give thanks to the LORD.
This is the gate of the LORD;
the righteous shall enter through it.
I thank you that you have answered me
and have become my salvation.
The stone that the builders rejected
has become the chief cornerstone.
This is the LORD's doing;
it is marvelous in our eyes.
This is the day that the LORD has made;
let us rejoice and be glad in it.

Save us, we beseech you, O LORD!
O LORD, we beseech you, give us success!
Blessed is the one who comes in the name of the LORD.
We bless you from the house of the LORD.
The LORD is God, and he has given us light.
Bind the festal procession with branches,
up to the horns of the altar.
You are my God, and I will give thanks to you;
you are my God, I will extol you.
O give thanks to the LORD, for he is good,
for his steadfast love endures forever.

MAUNDY THURSDAY
(Tenebrae Service)

- **THE EXTINGUISHING OF EACH OF SEVEN CANDLES**

- **ORGAN PRELUDE**

- **CALL TO WORSHIP and OPENING PRAYERS**

On this day our Lord went again to Jerusalem. In the evening in the Upper Room, He washed the feet of the disciples and instituted the Sacrament of His Body and Blood. He spoke words of comfort and peace, gave the promise of the coming of the Holy Spirit, and made the great intercession.
    In the Garden of Gethsemane He endured His agony. Betrayed by Judas and arrested by His enemies, He was taken to prison and to judgment.
    Compassionate and saving God, assist us by the Spirit that we may approach with reverence our meditation on the actions of Jesus to give us forgiveness, life and immortality. As we come to your table with reverence, Lord Jesus, enable us to confirm our discipleship and to renew our vows of loyalty to you.
    Be present to us in the breaking of the bread and the receiving of the cup. Join us with all your people who remember you around the table. Be with those who are finding life hard and faith difficult that they may rediscover you and be of good courage. Hear us as we pray in the words our Savior Christ has taught us: Our Father . . .

THE FINAL CONFLICT BEGINS   Mark 14:1-11
    * Wicked Plans — Mark 14:11
    HYMN: O Come And Mourn With Me A While

THE LAST SUPPER   Mark 14:12-25
    HYMN: 'Twas On That Night When Doomed To Know
    ** HOLY COMMUNION (Actions at the table may be synchronized
       with the words of the hymn above.)

PROPHECIES AND PROMISES   Mark 14:26-31
    * False Promises — Mark 14:31
    HYMN: When We Are Tempted To Deny Your Son
       — David Romig

A PLACE CALLED GETHSEMANE   Mark 14:32-52
   *Fearful Desertion — Mark 14:50
   HYMN: Go To Dark Gethsemane

TRIAL AT THE HIGH PRIEST'S HOUSE   Mark 14:53-72
   * Cowardly Denial — Mark 14:72
   HYMN: In The Hour Of Trial

TRIAL BEFORE THE GOVERNOR   Mark 15:1-20
   *Human Brutality — Mark 15:19
   HYMN: Ah, Holy Jesus, How Have You Offended?

THE CRUCIFIXION   Mark 15:21-39
   *Divine-Human Forsakenness — Mark 15:37
   HYMN: O Sacred Head Now Wounded

THE BURIAL   Mark 15:40-47
   *The Darkness Of Death — Mark 15:46
   HYMN: Were You There When They Crucified
      My Lord?

- **THE BENEDICTION** (Quiet departure)

- **POSTLUDE**

* Extinguish one candle
** Consider celebrating at a table surrounded by thirteen chairs. Have a place card with the name of a disciple in front of each chair.

EASTER

Acts 10:34-43 or Isaiah 25:6-9
1 Corinthians 15:1-11
or Acts 10:34-43

Psalm 118:1-2, 14-24
John 20:1-18
or Mark 16:1-8

- **CALL TO WORSHIP** (responsively)
This is the day on which the Lord has acted:
let us exult and rejoice in it.
We shall not die,
but live to proclaim the works of the Lord.

- **PRAYER OF CONFESSION**
God of the sabbath rest, God of Easter Sunday, God of everyday hear our confession. Embarrassment often closes our mouths, so we are often reluctant to share unusual experiences that doubters will question and cast aspersions on our sanity. Death mystifies us, but to be a witness of a resurrection would dumbfound us also. There is something fearsome about death and grievous in the separation it brings between the living and the dead. We want to overcome our doubts about resurrection. Help us to receive the witness of the apostles concerning the new creation begun after the Sabbath was ended and another first day of your creation began, for the sake of him you raised from death, Jesus Christ our Lord. Amen.

- **DECLARATION OF GOD'S FORGIVENESS**
Hear the Good News, brothers and sisters, ~~through which you are being saved,~~ that Christ died for our sins in accordance with the scriptures, and that he was buried, and that he was raised on the third day in accordance with the scriptures, and that he appeared to his disciples. Friends, believe the Good News! In Jesus Christ, we are forgiven.

- **EXHORTATION**
~~As Jesus said to his disciples:~~ "Go into all the world and proclaim the good news to the whole creation. The one who believes and is baptized will be saved; ~~but the one who does not believe will be condemned~~..."

- **PRAYER OF THE DAY**
Jesus of Nazareth, crucified Mortal, resurrected Christ, send us also to your whole creation with voices filled with the joy of faith and the message of eternal salvation from your cross and empty tomb, that others may share our Easter surprise and not be afraid of death. Amen.

• **PRAYER OF THANKSGIVING**
Giver of banquets, Dryer of Tears, Mover of Stone, we love your feast of bread and wine because it is to us the promise of life forever. We know how rare is the wine you make in the winepress of the cross, and from what wheat is stoneground the Bread of Life. All thanks and praise be given to you for you give us yourself. You have made your salvation known to us in Jesus of Nazareth, crucified and risen from the dead. You move the stone of death from the tomb of Jesus and the pall that shrouds every coffin. You will deliver us from the power of death and with gentleness wipe away the tears of our partings. Who can compare to you, in generosity in gentleness, in generating and re-generating life? Alleluia! Amen!

• **PRAYER OF DEDICATION**
Whatever we bring, our hands are basically empty, O God, held out to receive the bounties of your grace. So what we bring we give to share with others and to return with them to your table to respond in thanksgiving here and now, hereafter in eternity; through Jesus Christ, our Risen Lord. Amen.

• **PSALM 118:1-2, 14-24**
O give thanks to the LORD, for he is good;
his steadfast love endures forever!
Let Israel say, "His steadfast love endures forever."
The LORD is my strength and my might;
he has become my salvation.
There are glad songs of victory in the tents of the righteous:
"The right hand of the LORD does valiantly;
the right hand of the LORD is exalted;
the right hand of the LORD does valiantly."
I shall not die,
but I shall live, and recount the deeds of the LORD.
The LORD has punished me severely,
but he did not give me over to death.
Open to me the gates of righteousness,
that I may enter through them and give thanks to the LORD.
This is the gate of the LORD;
the righteous shall enter through it.
I thank you that you have answered me
and have become my salvation.
[All] *The stone that the builders rejected has become the chief cornerstone.*
This is the LORD's doing; it is marvelous in our eyes.
This is the day that the LORD has made; let us rejoice and be glad in it.

SECOND SUNDAY OF EASTER

Acts 4:32-35 Psalm 133
1 John 1:1-2:2 John 20:19-31

• CALL TO WORSHIP
Hear and read what is written down in the gospel of John in order that you may believe that Jesus is the Messiah, the son of God and that through your faith in him you may have life.

• PRAYER OF CONFESSION
God of all worlds, Easter Victor, Victorious Spirit, though we are declared to be victors over the godless world, we often feel doubtful and defeated. We are too prone to go by our feelings and not to accept the witness of the apostles, believing his victory to be our victory over sin and death. Victorious Spirit, overcome our doubts and fears as we read and hear the apostolic witness. Increase our love as well, for we need to love others who are not as lovable as Jesus Christ. Amen.

• DECLARATION OF GOD'S FORGIVENESS
Hear the Good News! The victory that defeats the world is our faith; for who is victor over evil, but the one who believes that Jesus is the Son of God. Friends, believe the Good News! In Jesus Christ, we are forgiven.

• EXHORTATION
Obey the commands of the God you love and you will love God's children too.

• PRAYER OF THE DAY
God of earth and heaven, Christ of the cross and resurrection, Spirit of creation and re-creation, grant us the blessing that you promise to those who believe in the risen Christ without visible and tangible proof of his victory over death. Amen.

• PRAYER OF THANKSGIVING
God of the living, Conqueror of death, Spirit of Love, we give thanks and praise for every victory you give us over our fears, our failures, our selfishness; for the courage to do what would otherwise be impossible for us; and for the companionship of those who work with us in common enterprises. We are grateful for the examples of those who have gone before us, who have given us noble experiments in unselfish service and modeled the selflessness we do not often practice. We praise your giving,

your living, your loving, God above us, God beside us, God within us. Amen.

• PRAYER OF DEDICATION
Living, loving, giving Spirit, surprise us with the joy of living, that overcomes any pain in parting with our money, or any pride in giving ourselves. Amen.

• PSALM 133
How very good and pleasant it is when kindred live together in unity!
It is like the precious oil on the head,
running down upon the beard,
on the beard of Aaron,
running down over the collar of his robes.
It is like the dew of Hermon,
which falls on the mountains of Zion.
For there the LORD ordained his blessing,
life forevermore.

THIRD SUNDAY OF EASTER

Acts 3:12-19　　　　　　　　　　　　　　　　　　　　　Psalm 4
1 John 3:1-7　　　　　　　　　　　　　　　　　　　　Luke 24:36b-48

• CALL TO WORSHIP
God is everywhere. Pause here to be armed with the power from above. This is God's promised gift.

• PRAYER OF CONFESSION
God of all pilgrims, of all children of the faithful, of all wrestlers with the truth, we confess our complicity with many of the evils of society as well as our repentance of some of them in the strength you have given us in the church. We are of the same humanity that repudiated the suffering Messiah. We are of the repenting community whose sins are wiped out. We need to know you more truly so that your divine love may come to perfection in us, through the Spirit of the Risen Christ. Amen.

• DECLARATION OF GOD'S FORGIVENESS
Hear the Good News! We have one to plead our cause with the Divine Parent, Jesus Christ who is just and the remedy for the defilement of our sins, not our sin only but the sins of all the world. Friends, believe the Good News! In Jesus Christ, we are forgiven.

• EXHORTATION
Bind yourself to love as Christ loved.

• PRAYER OF THE DAY
Self-giving God, continue to give us your promised gift that we may be empowered to obey your commands and be faithful proclaimers of the forgiveness of sins to all nations, through the dying and rising Messiah, and his gift with the Father of the Spirit of Love. Amen.

• PRAYER OF THANKSGIVING
God above us, leading us to exaltation; God beneath us, lifting us out of degradation; God around us, attracting our adoration; God before us leading us to perfection; God behind us guarding us from discouragement. Where would we be without you? What future could we anticipate without your leading? We worship you, God of all nations. We follow you, loving Messiah. We welcome you, indwelling Spirit. Amen.

• PRAYER OF DEDICATION
Risen Christ, give us faith to see that it is into your hands we offer our gifts and that it is your feet we follow when we go out so serve others in the Spirit of love. Amen.

• PSALM 4
Answer me when I call, O God of my right!
You gave me room when I was in distress.
Be gracious to me, and hear my prayer.
How long, you people, shall my honor suffer shame?
How long will you love vain words,
and seek after lies?
But know that the LORD has set apart the faithful for himself;
the LORD hears when I call to him.
When you are disturbed, do not sin;
ponder it on your beds, and be silent.
Offer right sacrifices,
and put your trust in the LORD.
There are many who say, "O that we might see some good!
Let the light of your face shine on us, O LORD!"
You have put gladness in my heart
more than when their grain and wine abound.
I will both lie down and sleep in peace;
for you alone, O LORD, make me lie down in safety.

FOURTH SUNDAY OF EASTER

Acts 4:5-12　　　　　　　　　　　　　　　　　　Psalm 23
1 John 3:16-24　　　　　　　　　　　　　　　John 10:11-18

• CALL TO WORSHIP
Approach God with confidence. Do what God approves and ask what you will.

• PRAYER OF CONFESSION
Creator, Repairer, Sustainer of consciences, we need your continued attention, because at times our consciences are dull or numb and need to be set true again, and sensitive to what should bother us. Confrontation of painful truth may be what we need to jolt us into action that is appropriate for the children of God. Forgive our avoidance of what we should do and our neglect of what we started but have not finished, for the sake of Jesus, who finished what you sent him to do. Amen.

• DECLARATION OF GOD'S FORGIVENESS
Hear the Good News! Jesus, our Good Shepherd, laid down his life for us, his sheep, that we might live. Friends, believe the Good News! In Jesus Christ, we are forgiven.

• EXHORTATION
Give allegiance to God's son, Jesus Christ, and love one another as he commanded.

• PRAYER OF THE DAY
Good Shepherd, hasten the day when it will be clear that there is one flock and one shepherd, when above all the discordant voices of our times, your voice will be heard loud and clear. Amen.

• PRAYER OF THANKSGIVING
Bountiful Host, what a profusion of good things you have created for us to enjoy. Your provisions for the sustenance of the body and the spirit are beyond measure, our cup overflows. Your promises are sure and we expect your goodness and mercy to nurture us all our days and bring us to the time and place where we know your presence even more intimately than today. Today and every day, may we remember to express our thanksgiving. Amen.

• PRAYER OF DEDICATION
Actions are what you look for, Bishop of the church, so let these words and these offerings signify what we will do to serve you. Amen.

• PSALM 23
The LORD is my shepherd, I shall not want.
He makes me lie down in green pastures;
he leads me beside still waters; he restores my soul.
He leads me in right paths for his name's sake.
Even though I walk through the darkest valley,
I fear no evil; for you are with me;
your rod and your staff — they comfort me.
You prepare a table before me in the presence of my enemies;
you anoint my head with oil; my cup overflows.
Surely goodness and mercy shall follow me all the days of my life,
and I shall dwell in the house of the LORD my whole life long.

FIFTH SUNDAY OF EASTER

Acts 8:26-40
1 John 4:7-21

Psalm 22:25-31
John 15:1-8

• CALL TO WORSHIP
Seek the Sovereign of all nations. Praise God and be in good heart for ever.

• PRAYER OF CONFESSION
Divine Gardener, you have planted the true Vine in our world and sustain living branches by the Spirit. We confess that we do not always readily receive into our fellowship those you send to us. We are suspicious of those who seem different or whose sincerity we question. We may fear that we will be replaced, forgetting that you want your church to grow like a healthy vineyard, well-pruned of dead wood and producing the fruits of the Spirit. Forgive us if we in pride seek to take over your role as Gardener, discontent to be but branches of your true vine, Jesus Christ. Amen.

• DECLARATION OF GOD'S FORGIVENESS
Hear the Good News! God is love, and God's love was disclosed to us in the sending of the divine Son into the world to bring us life, the remedy of the defilement of our sins. Friends, believe the Good News! In Jesus Christ, we are forgiven.

• EXHORTATION
Remain united with the Vine, Jesus Christ. No branch can bear fruit by itself.

• PRAYER OF THE DAY
Divine Vine Tender, so prune and tie us as branches of the vine that, being rid of all unfruitfulness and directed by the commands of Christ, we may bear fruit to your glory and our joy. Amen.

• PRAYER OF THANKSGIVING
God of all nations, Universal Christ, Including Spirit, we praise your name and names for the love that embraces us and the ties that bind us together as a church across all lines of race and class, across the centuries from the beginning until now, across all stages of human growth from childhood to old age. Our baptism, by whatever mode, has joined us to you in a living relationship that spans all human differences and will survive beyond the grave. We give you hearty thanks and unceasing praise for your love is beyond all imagining. Amen.

• **PRAYER OF DEDICATION**
Giving God, receive what we give to you in response to the loving gift of Jesus, your divine Child, so that we may be assured that you know of our love for you however small in comparison with your gifts to us. Amen.

• **PSALM 22:25-31**
From you comes my praise in the great congregation;
my vows I will pay before those who fear him.
The poor shall eat and be satisfied;
those who seek him shall praise the LORD.
May your hearts live forever!
All the ends of the earth shall remember and turn to the LORD;
and all the families of the nations shall worship before him.
For dominion belongs to the LORD,
and he rules over the nations.
To him, indeed, shall all who sleep in the earth bow down;
before him shall bow all who go down to the dust, and
I shall live for him.
Posterity will serve him;
future generations will be told about the Lord,
and proclaim his deliverance to a people yet unborn,
saying that he has done it.

SIXTH SUNDAY OF EASTER

Acts 10:44-48 Psalm 98
1 John 5:1-6 John 15:9-17

• CALL TO WORSHIP
Sing praises in God's honor with the harp and the music of the psaltery. With trumpet and echoing horn acclaim the presence of God, our Sovereign.

• PRAYER OF CONFESSION
God without favorites, from every nation you accept the person who reveres you and does what is right, but we do what is unacceptable to you. We need the forgiveness and spiritual healing that you offer us in Jesus of Nazareth and the Holy Spirit. Free us from the oppression of evil that we may be free to worship you with great joy and, bearing witness to Christ crucified and raised from the dead may see the baptism of others who put their trust in his name. Amen.

• DECLARATION OF GOD'S FORGIVENESS
Hear the Good News! You are of God's family and the One inspiring you is greater than the evil spirit inspiring the godless world. Friends, believe the Good News. In Jesus Christ, we are forgiven.

• EXHORTATION
Do not trust any and every spirit in the world, for there are many prophets falsely inspired and not from God, and do not acknowledge that Jesus Christ has come in humanity from God.

• PRAYER OF THE DAY
Loving Parent, commanding Presence, keep us in your love so that in humble acceptance of our election we may accomplish our appointed task in the freedom of friendship rather than the duty of servitude, loving and serving as Jesus did. Amen.

• PRAYER OF THANKSGIVING
For all judges who are committed to justice as you are, O God, we give you thanks, trusting in the final victory of goodness. For all prophets who are inspired by your Spirit of truth, anointed One, intent on being faithful witnesses to you, we praise your name, Jesus of Nazareth. For all musicians, who receiving your Spirit, Universal One, celebrate the beauty of creation, the baptism of your grace, the unity of your church, we express our gratitude and join them as we can with voices and instruments of all

kinds. We worship you with all kindred souls in every time and place with humility and love and obedience. Amen.

• **PRAYER OF DEDICATION**
We serve you, Great God, with whatever we have, with our financial resources, with our musical skills, with our voices and our pens, with hands that can be folded in prayer and open in the service of others, with our feet that bring us here and take us out again into the world for which you gave your Son Jesus in life and resurrection. Amen.

• **PSALM 98**
O sing to the LORD a new song,
for he has done marvelous things.
His right hand and his holy arm have gotten him victory.
The LORD has made known his victory;
he has revealed his vindication in the sight of the nations.
He has remembered his steadfast love and faithfulness to the house of Israel.
All the ends of the earth have seen the victory of our God.
Make a joyful noise to the LORD, all the earth;
break forth into joyous song and sing praises.
Sing praises to the LORD with the lyre,
with the lyre and the sound of melody.
With trumpets and the sound of the horn
make a joyful noise before the King, the LORD.
Let the sea roar, and all that fills it;
the world and those who live in it.
Let the floods clap their hands;
let the hills sing together for joy
at the presence of the LORD,
for he is coming to judge the earth.
He will judge the world with righteousness,
and the peoples with equity.

ASCENSION DAY

Acts 1:1-11
Ephesians 1:15-23
Psalm 47
Luke 24:44-53

• CALL TO WORSHIP and INVOCATION
Let us worship God.
Let us pray
    that our inward eyes may be illumined
    that we may know what is the hope to which God calls us
    that we may learn how vast are the resources of the
        Spirit's power
    that we may value the wealth of the heritage that we share
        with Christ.

• SILENT PRAYER

• PRAYER OF CONFESSION
God of Moses, God of the Messiah, God of the church, forgive the doubts that plague us, the questions as to your timetable for history, the fears that the events of our time are beyond all control, even yours. Excuse our slowness in fulfilling our mission of proclaiming to all nations the name of Jesus and the repentance which brings forgiveness of sins. We need such forgiveness ourselves, for we have not properly acknowledged your majesty and power, nor received your gracious enablement to complete your work in the world. Have patience with us and the whole body of the church of which Jesus Christ is the head, in his name. Amen.

• DECLARATION OF GOD'S FORGIVENESS
Hear the Good News! Jesus sent his Father's promised gift of the Holy Spirit to arm us with power from above. Friends, believe the Good News. In Jesus Christ we are forgiven.

• EXHORTATION
Keep your minds open to understand the Scriptures, for all that was written in the Law of Moses and in the prophets and in the psalms were bound to be fulfilled in Jesus Christ. Be prepared to be a witness to all these things.

• PRAYER OF THE DAY
God of our Lord Jesus Christ, All-glorious Parent, bless us with such insightful faith that we may worship you with great joy, spending in your house enough time to prepare us to be your witnesses everywhere in the world, by the power of the Holy Spirit. Amen.

- **PRAYER OF THANKSGIVING**
We praise you, Lord Christ, ascended to the right hand of Divine Sovereignty. Since your mother, Mary, bore you, you have been resplendent in holiness. The symbol for your power is the empty cross, for you have vanquished sin and death. In the Spirit you give your church powers of wisdom and vision. Thanks to you, Son of God, we are given knowledge of the Father, and thanks to you, Divine Spirit, we are given knowledge of the Son, and the inspiration to witness before the world the good news entrusted to the church. Amen.

- **PRAYER OF DEDICATION**
Our resources are limited, Lord God, but yours are not. What we give is multiplied beyond measure when we open ourselves to being used by the Spirit enlivening the church of the beloved Son. Amen.

- **PSALM 47:1-9**
Clap your hands, all you peoples;
shout to God with loud songs of joy.
For the LORD, the Most High, is awesome,
a great king over all the earth.
He subdued peoples under us,
and nations under our feet.
He chose our heritage for us,
the pride of Jacob whom he loves.
God has gone up with a shout,
the LORD with the sound of a trumpet.
Sing praises to God, sing praises;
sing praises to our King, sing praises.
For God is the king of all the earth;
sing praises with a psalm.
God is king over the nations;
God sits on his holy throne.
The princes of the peoples gather
as the people of the God of Abraham.
For the shields of the earth belong to God;
he is highly exalted.

SEVENTH SUNDAY OF EASTER

Acts 1:15-17, 21-26 Psalm 1
1 John 5:9-13 John 17:6-19

• **CALL TO WORSHIP** (responsively)
How awesome is God most high,
great sovereign over all the earth!
Christ has gone up with shouts of acclamation
to the right hand of the throne of the eternal.
Let us acclaim our God with shouts of joy,
praising Monarch and Prince with psalms and fanfares.

• **PRAYER OF CONFESSION**
God invisible in majesty, God incognito in the world, namesharing God, how could we know you more fully than as you have revealed yourself in the One who came into the world but has ascended again into the holiest place. We need to be consecrated by the truth, since we are too ready to compromise it rather than be treated as strange, as Jesus often was. Forgive us if we have been ashamed to confess the name of Christ and denied the power of that name to cleanse us from the defilement of sin and to keep us from further exposure to the evil One who would lead us astray. Deliver us from evil through the power of the Spirit imparted to us in Christ's name. Amen.

• **DECLARATION OF GOD'S FORGIVENESS**
Hear the Good News! God loved us by sending his Son as the remedy for the defilement of our sins. Friends, believe the Good News. In Jesus Christ, we are forgiven.

• **EXHORTATION**
If God thus loved us, dear friends, we in turn are bound to love one another.

• **PRAYER OF THE DAY**
Holy and powerful Parent, while we are still in the world, remind us of the power of the name you share with us through Jesus Christ, so that, truly honoring that name by our behavior, we may be kept from the evil one and come at last to your presence no stranger to your love and grace. Amen.

• **PRAYER OF THANKSGIVING**
God, loving and inseparable; Son of God, loving and sendable; Spirit of God, loving and impartable; we have come to know and believe the love

which you have for us. We are grateful for the love we share in the family of Jesus Christ, as his brothers and sisters. Your love is being brought to perfection within us through our need to seek and grant forgiveness, through our search for the full and true meaning of your Word, in the struggle to understand one another and overcome misunderstanding. For all experiences of growth and every increased capacity to love as you love, we express our thanksgiving. For every discovery of new kinship in the Spirit, we rejoice with great joy, as your family continues to grow locally and internationally. All praise to you, all-loving God. Amen.

• PRAYER OF DEDICATION
Eternal Parent, as you sent your Son into the world to show your love, send us also from this place to where our witness to the truth will also be an expression of your love, through Jesus Christ our Savior. Amen.

• PSALM 1
Happy are those who do not follow the advice of the wicked,
or take the path that sinners tread, or sit in the seat of scoffers;
but their delight is in the law of the LORD,
and on his law they meditate day and night.
They are like trees planted by streams of water,
which yield their fruit in its season, and their leaves do not wither.
In all that they do, they prosper.
The wicked are not so, but are like chaff that the wind drives away.
Therefore the wicked will not stand in the judgment,
nor sinners in the congregation of the righteous;
for the LORD watches over the way of the righteous,
but the way of the wicked will perish.

PENTECOST

Acts 2:1-21 or Ezekiel 37:1-14　　　　　　Psalm 104:24-34, 35b
Romans 8:22-27 or Acts 2:1-21　　　　　　John 15:26-27; 16:4b-15

• **CALL TO WORSHIP**
Look to our Creator who gives breath to all breathing creatures and the Spirit to all praying beings.

• **PRAYER OF CONFESSION**
Unseen Parent, Departed Brother, Promised Counselor, we admit that we have not always confessed that we have done what is wrong. We do not always seek the truth to know and do what is right. Though we should declare our faults and failings out of sheer love and trust, we more often confess out of threat of future judgment. Forgive indifference and noncommittal discipleship with too much drift and very little direction. We need the intensity and intentionality of your Son Jesus; through the promised Spirit. Amen.

• **DECLARATION OF GOD'S FORGIVENESS**
Hear the Good News! Everyone who invokes Jesus Christ by name shall be saved. Friends, believe the Good News. In Jesus Christ, we are forgiven.

• **EXHORTATION**
Be open to God who will pour out the Spirit on all humanity, so that our children will prophesy, the old will dream dreams and the young see visions.

• **PRAYER OF THE DAY**
Spirit of truth, guide us into all truth, so that we may know where wrong and right and judgment lie, and in knowing what is coming, stand with you and not with the Prince of this world who already stands condemned. Amen.

• **PRAYER OF THANKSGIVING**
Doer-of-great-things, glorified-Truth-Teller, truthful Advocate, what great things you do and promise, and fulfill. We are continually amazed at the speech you give the speechless, the power you give to the powerless, the meaning you give to those whose lives have seemed meaningless. We live in anticipation of what your loving Spirit can still do as people are open to the gifts your Spirit will give in and through the church of Jesus Christ. We glorify you, Father, Son and mothering Spirit. Amen.

- **PRAYER OF DEDICATION**
You, too, are mind, and body and spirit, O God. We bring our offerings to support the church's ministry of learning and doing and praying to the glory of your name. Amen.

- **PSALM 104: 24-34, 35b**
O LORD, how manifold are your works!
*In wisdom you have made them all;
the earth is full of your creatures.*
Yonder is the sea, great and wide,
*creeping things innumerable are there,
living things both small and great.*
There go the ships,
and Leviathan that you formed to sport in it.
These all look to you to give them their food in due season;
*when you give to them, they gather it up;
when you open your hand, they are filled with good things.*
When you hide your face, they are dismayed;
when you take away their breath, they die and return to their dust.
When you send forth your spirit, they are created;
and you renew the face of the ground.
May the glory of the LORD endure forever;
may the LORD rejoice in his works —
who looks on the earth and it trembles,
who touches the mountains and they smoke.
I will sing to the LORD as long as I live;
I will sing praise to my God while I have being.
May my meditation be pleasing to him,
for I rejoice in the LORD.
Bless the LORD, O my soul.
Praise the LORD!

TRINITY SUNDAY

Isaiah 6:1-8　　　　　　　　　　　　　　　　　　　　　　Psalm 29
Romans 8:12-17　　　　　　　　　　　　　　　　　　　　John 3:1-17

• **CALL TO WORSHIP**
Search for a vision of God. Listen for the voices of God's messengers. Enlist in the embassy of God.

• **PRAYER OF CONFESSION**
Three-times-holy One, our best parenting is but a shadow of your giving and caring for us. Our devotion to brothers and sisters can hardly be compared to the self-giving of Jesus Christ, Our Brother. The most understanding and forgiving family spirit we share is hardly comparable to the unity in love which is your nature. We are lost if we flee your loving discipline. We are estranged if we deny your Son Jesus. We are orphaned if we are not bound to you by the Spirit. Mercifully keep us in your family through Jesus Christ our Savior. Amen.

• **DECLARATION OF GOD'S FORGIVENESS**
Hear the Good News! Our lower nature has no claim upon us. We are not obliged to live on that level. All who are moved by the Spirit of God are children of God. Friends, believe the Good News! In Jesus Christ, we are forgiven.

• **EXHORTATION**
By the Spirit put to death all the base pursuits of the body, and you will live in the freedom of the children of God.

• **PRAYER OF THE DAY**
Paternal God, Brotherly Christ, Motherly Spirit, give us to see in your gospel the sign of your presence with and work through the Christ, that seeing the evidence of your power, then and now, we may experience a rebirth of the Spirit, enabled to see and enter the place where you alone rule uncontested. Amen.

• **PRAYER OF THANKSGIVING**
Glorious God, you fill the universe with majestic beauty and flowers in unexpected places. Holy God, you hallow awesome sanctuaries humbling us with the sense of our smallness and our sins. Sanctifying Spirit, you purify us, removing our iniquities and renewing us as if childlike in innocence, starting life again. We worship you with songs and verses, new

songs and old songs with old instruments and new instruments of music, with processions and dances, with liturgy and daily work. All thanks be given to you for your great gifts of nature and grace, unseen Creator, First-born of creation, re-creating Spirit. Amen.

• **PRAYER OF DEDICATION**
Understanding Parent, though we rejoice to be joint-heirs of splendor with Jesus Christ, is it possible that we lose if we do not give until it hurts? Teach us how to share the sufferings of the Christ, for his name's sake Amen.

• **PSALM 29**
Ascribe to the LORD, O heavenly beings,
ascribe to the LORD glory and strength.
Ascribe to the LORD the glory of his name;
worship the LORD in holy splendor.
The voice of the LORD is over the waters;
the God of glory thunders, the LORD, over mighty waters.
The voice of the LORD is powerful;
the voice of the LORD is full of majesty.
The voice of the LORD breaks the cedars;
the LORD breaks the cedars of Lebanon.
He makes Lebanon skip like a calf,
and Sirion like a young wild ox.
The voice of the LORD flashes forth flames of fire.
The voice of the LORD shakes the wilderness;
the LORD shakes the wilderness of Kadesh.
The voice of the LORD causes the oaks to whirl,
and strips the forest bare; and in his temple all say, "Glory!"
The LORD sits enthroned over the flood;
the LORD sits enthroned as king forever.
May the LORD give strength to his people!
May the LORD bless his people with peace!

PROPER 4

1 Samuel 3:1-10, (11-20) Psalm 139:1-6, 13-18
2 Corinthians 4:5-12 Mark 2:23-3:6

• CALL TO WORSHIP
Jesus Christ is Lord and the Light of God. Come to the Light. Come to the light which shines out of darkness.

• PRAYER OF CONFESSION
Holy God, devout Christ, sanctifying Spirit, cleanse our speech from any trivial use of your hallowed name. Save us from attributing to you the hatreds and curses that issue from our anger whether justified or not. May our restraint turn others from the blasphemous use of your name and the desecration of what is holy. Hallowed be your name, Father, Son, and Holy Spirit. Amen.

• DECLARATION OF GOD'S FORGIVENESS
Hear the Good News! The death that Jesus died in us reveals also the life that Jesus lives. Friends, believe the Good News! In Jesus Christ, we are forgiven.

• EXHORTATION
Keep a day of rest from work for everyone in your household so that you can give thanks to God for freedom and all of God's great gifts.

• PRAYER OF THE DAY
Cure us, healing Christ, on this and every day of rest, that being restored in body, mind and spirit, we may do what is good, learn what is helpful and return to our daily work invigorated and inspired. Amen.

• PRAYER OF THANKSGIVING
Creator of light, we rejoice in the sunrise of each day, whether veiled with clouds or brilliant with the colors of morning. We celebrate your glory revealed in the face of Jesus Christ. Whether in the sombre light of Good Friday or the bright glory of resurrection morning, we live in the light your Spirit spreads in our minds and hearts, thankful for new understanding of your purposes for us, for fresh courage to face adversity, for new moral life as our sins are put to death. We praise you, Light above us, Light beside us, Light within us. Amen.

• **PRAYER OF DEDICATION**
God of power, you generously share your divine power with us in the plain earthenware that we are as the church of your beloved Son, Jesus. Our offering of time, money, and ourselves are to provide such humble media for the use of your Spirit, in the name of Jesus Christ. Amen.

• **PSALM 139:1-6, 13-18**
O LORD, you have searched me and known me.
You know when I sit down and when I rise up;
you discern my thoughts from far away.
You search out my path and my lying down,
and are acquainted with all my ways.
Even before a word is on my tongue,
O LORD, you know it completely.
You hem me in, behind and before,
and lay your hand upon me.
Such knowledge is too wonderful for me;
it is so high that I cannot attain it.
For it was you who formed my inward parts;
you knit me together in my mother's womb.
I praise you, for I am fearfully and wonderfully made.
Wonderful are your works; that I know very well.
My frame was not hidden from you, when I was being made in secret, intricately woven in the depths of the earth.
Your eyes beheld my unformed substance. In your book were written all the days that were formed for me, when none of them as yet existed.
How weighty to me are your thoughts, O God!
How vast is the sum of them!
I try to count them — they are more than the sand;
I come to the end — I am still with you.

PROPER 5

1 Samuel 8:4-11, (12-15), 16-20, (11:14-15)   Psalm 138
2 Corinthians 4:13-5:1   Mark 3:20-35

- **CALL TO WORSHIP**
Let us call upon God most high to fulfill the divine purpose for us, sending us truth and love that never fails.

- **PRAYER OF CONFESSION**
King Eternal, Prince of Peace, Royal Spirit, teach us to make the distinction between obedience to your will and the laws of human government. We confess that we are too often content to live by human law and not the higher commands of our Lord Jesus Christ. While we seek to be good citizens of the United States of America, enable us to abide by the even higher standards of your realm of truth and goodness; through Jesus Christ our Lord. Amen.

- **DECLARATION OF GOD'S FORGIVENESS**
Hear the Good News! The One who raised Christ Jesus to life will with Jesus raise us too, and bring us to his presence. Friends, believe the Good News. In Jesus Christ, we are forgiven.

- **EXHORTATION**
Fix your eyes not on the things that are seen, but on the things that are unseen. What is seen passes away. What is unseen is eternal.

- **PRAYER OF THE DAY**
Creator of all, from Eden to the end of the world, watch over your people of the promise, forgiving our disobedience, that we may drink the new wine with all who trust your grace in Jesus Christ our Savior. Amen.

- **PRAYER OF THANKSGIVING**
God of grace, from the old world to the new, from the Atlantic to the Pacific, there is increasing thanksgiving to you as your merciful power raises us from death to life, bridging the gap that has separated us from you, and spanning the gulf between the transient and the eternal. By the Spirit you are renewing our inner nature every day until we shall be radiant with your glory, in Jesus Christ, our Light and Light of the world. Amen.

• **PRAYER OF DEDICATION**
Head of this household, our offerings are an expression of our commitment to do your will and be the brothers and sisters of Jesus Christ. Amen.

• **PSALM 138:1-8**
I give you thanks, O LORD, with my whole heart;
before the gods I sing your praise;
I bow down toward your holy temple and give thanks to your name for your steadfast love and your faithfulness;
for you have exalted your name and your word above everything.
On the day I called, you answered me,
you increased my strength of soul.
All the kings of the earth shall praise you, O LORD,
for they have heard the words of your mouth.
They shall sing of the ways of the LORD,
for great is the glory of the LORD.
For though the LORD is high, he regards the lowly;
but the haughty he perceives from far away.
Though I walk in the midst of trouble,
you preserve me against the wrath of my enemies;
you stretch out your hand,
and your right hand delivers me.
The LORD will fulfill his purpose for me;
your steadfast love, O LORD, endures forever.
Do not forsake the work of your hands.

PROPER 6

1 Samuel 15:34 - 16:13
2 Corinthians 5:6-10, (11-13), 14-17

Psalm 20
Mark 4:26-34

• CALL TO WORSHIP
Come to Christ the great story teller and he will teach you in public and in private the meaning of life.

• PRAYER OF CONFESSION
God of here and there, Judge of now and then, though you are beyond our line of sight and we must walk by faith, we believe that you are always aware of us and what we do. We know we are on trial, being tested, our conduct under your scrutiny. We confess that our behavior is neither as good nor as bad as it might be. We are not as ambitious for your acceptance as we might be. As exiles, we are anxious to leave the testing grounds behind us, to live with you beyond all danger of failure. Forgive all badness for the sake of Jesus Christ and the goodness he shares with us. Amen.

• DECLARATION OF GOD'S FORGIVENESS
Hear the Good News! Those who are planted in the house of the Lord will flourish in the courts of our God, eager to declare that the Lord is just in whom there is no unrighteousness. Friends, believe the Good News! In Jesus Christ, we are forgiven.

• EXHORTATION
Never cease to be confident, that when we leave our home in the body that we will go to live with the Lord. Live now to be acceptable to the Christ in all you do.

• PRAYER OF THE DAY
Public Teacher, private Tutor, increase our ability to receive all that you teach, so that as your disciples we may be able to understand all that you will explain and follow you wherever you lead. Amen.

• PRAYER OF THANKSGIVING
Sovereign Forester, you cut down the proud tree to leave room for the hidden tree to grow. You nurture the seedling and give life again to the tree that appears to be dead. Your wisdom is beyond our understanding. You bring goodness to maturity in the most unlikely places and in most mysterious ways. Who could believe that your church could grow from

twelve to five hundred and from thousands to millions? That your rule should spread from Palestine to the ends of the earth? We are thankful that your realm grows in depth and ever-extending sweep, and that the end of history has its beginning is in your hands. All praise to you, Planter and Reaper, God of yesterday and tomorrow, Christ of our youth and our old age, unfailing Spirit of Life. Amen.

• **PRAYER OF DEDICATION**
God of all living things, landscape your world with the spreading shrubs and trees of your church that all things beautiful and good may flourish and add glory to your name. Amen.

• **PSALM 20:1-9**
The LORD answer you in the day of trouble!
The name of the God of Jacob protect you!
May he send you help from the sanctuary,
and give you support from Zion.
May he remember all your offerings,
and regard with favor your burnt sacrifices.
May he grant you your heart's desire,
and fulfill all your plans.
May we shout for joy over your victory,
and in the name of our God set up our banners.
May the LORD fulfill all your petitions.
Now I know that the LORD will help his anointed;
he will answer him from his holy heaven
with mighty victories by his right hand.
Some take pride in chariots, and some in horses,
but our pride is in the name of the LORD our God.
They will collapse and fall,
but we shall rise and stand upright.
Give victory to the king, O LORD;
answer us when we call.

PROPER 7

1 Samuel 17:(1a, 4-11,19-23), 32-49   Psalm 9:9-20
or   or
1 Samuel 17:57-18:5, 10-16   Psalm 133
2 Corinthians 6:1-13   Mark 4:35-41

• CALL TO WORSHIP
God's name deserves our praise in this house and to the farthest bounds of the earth.

• PRAYER OF CONFESSION
Creator of the good, Recoverer of the good, Inspirer of the good, our grandest cities and our finest houses are at best pale shadows of the city of God. We have corrupted them with vice and violence and greed. We have only belatedly made more adequate provision for the handicapped. Forgive our failures in making our highest dreams come true, with the strength of justice, the humanity of compassion, the dignity of equality. It is not the City of David but the City of Christ that we need. Amen.

• DECLARATION OF GOD'S FORGIVENESS
Hear the Good News! God was in Christ reconciling the world to Godself, no longer holding our misdeeds against us. Friends, believe the Good News! In Jesus Christ, we are forgiven.

• EXHORTATION
As we work together with Christ, we urge you also not to accept the grace of God in vain.

• PRAYER OF THE DAY
Caring Creator and Leader, reassure us that the powers of nature are not beyond your control, nor the inner storms of our own nature beyond your quieting touch, so that we may trust you more fully and find the calm we need when circumstances threaten to swamp us. Amen.

• PRAYER OF THANKSGIVING
God of storm and calm, Christ of confusion and order, Spirit of gales and stillness, we are grateful to find you near whatever the weather of social or geographic circumstance. What enormous powers surround us, some that we can harness, others that we can only witness with awe. We are grateful for the camaraderie common danger may inspire among us and

for the special courage so often brought out by emergencies. We give special thanks for those who have come to our aid, not least, Christ our savior. Amen.

• PRAYER OF DEDICATION
Let our gifts, divine Reconciler, be a sign of our faith that you will still work through your church as a ministry of reconciliation in this troubled world. Amen.

• PSALM 9:9-20
The LORD is a stronghold for the oppressed,
a stronghold in times of trouble.
And those who know your name put their trust in you,
for you, O LORD, have not forsaken those who seek you.
Sing praises to the LORD, who dwells in Zion.
Declare his deeds among the peoples.
For he who avenges blood is mindful of them;
he does not forget the cry of the afflicted.
Be gracious to me, O LORD.
See what I suffer from those who hate me;
you are the one who lifts me up from the gates of death,
so that I may recount all your praises,
and, in the gates of daughter Zion, rejoice in your deliverance.
The nations have sunk in the pit that they made;
in the net that they hid has their own foot been caught.
The LORD has made himself known, he has executed judgment;
the wicked are snared in the work of their own hands.
The wicked shall depart to Sheol,
all the nations that forget God.
For the needy shall not always be forgotten,
nor the hope of the poor perish forever.
Rise up, O LORD! Do not let mortals prevail;
let the nations be judged before you.
Put them in fear, O LORD;
let the nations know that they are only human.

(or)

• **PSALM 133:1-3**
How very good and pleasant it is
when kindred live together in unity!
It is like the precious oil on the head, running down upon the beard,
on the beard of Aaron, running down over the collar of his robes.
It is like the dew of Hermon,
which falls on the mountains of Zion.
For there the LORD ordained his blessing,
life forevermore.

PROPER 8

2 Samuel 1:1, 17-27 Psalm 130
2 Corinthians 8:7-15 Mark 5:21-43

• **CALL TO WORSHIP**
Seek the face of the God of Israel and of Jesus to receive the blessing of God our Savior.

• **PRAYER OF CONFESSION**
God of death and life, of tragedy and comedy, of sorrow and joy, we confess our dismay at the grief and accident that you permit to happen in this world. We question the accident happening to the person whose intentions seem to be good and the good fortune that seems to attend those intent on mischief. We can not understand why some are healed miraculously and others are allowed to suffer almost endlessly. Forgive us if we permit our doubts to threaten our commitment to you through Jesus Christ. Amen.

• **DECLARATION OF GOD'S FORGIVENESS**
Hear the Good News! How generous our Lord Jesus Christ has been: he was rich, yet for your sake he became poor, so that we through his poverty might become rich. Friends, believe the Good News! In Jesus Christ, we are forgiven.

• **EXHORTATION**
Be rich in faith, speech, knowledge, and zeal of every kind. Show yourselves lavish in generous service.

• **PRAYER OF THE DAY**
Approachable God, may we touch you in faith and receive the cure of our spiritual and physical maladies so that we may live at peace and in freedom from what troubles us, through Jesus Christ our Savior. Amen.

• **PRAYER OF THANKSGIVING**
God of mystery, many of the things that you do are quite beyond any explanation. Other events move us to joy and dancing with music and many instruments. Let our music also express our questions as well as our affirmations that we may rejoice in all things whether in a minor or a major key. Give us joy also in our work both begun and finished with satisfaction. We offer our work and our charities as thanksgiving to you, in Jesus Christ. Amen.

- **PRAYER OF DEDICATION**

You accept, O God, what we have to give and do no expect us to give what we do not have or can not do. From what we possess and from the talents that we have may we give without stint. Amen.

- **PSALM 130:1-8**

Out of the depths I cry to you, O LORD.
Lord, hear my voice!
Let your ears be attentive to the voice of my supplications!
If you, O LORD, should mark iniquities, Lord, who could stand?
But there is forgiveness with you, so that you may be revered.
I wait for the LORD,
my soul waits, and in his word I hope;
my soul waits for the Lord more than those who watch for the morning,
more than those who watch for the morning.
O Israel, hope in the LORD!
For with the LORD there is steadfast love,
and with him is great power to redeem.
It is he who will redeem Israel from all its iniquities.

PROPER 9

2 Samuel 5:1-5, 9-10 Psalm 48
2 Corinthians 12:2-10 Mark 6:1-13

• CALL TO WORSHIP
Come to worship with an honest acknowledgment of your weaknesses, and the power of Christ will come and rest upon you.

• PRAYER OF CONFESSION
Sovereign of sovereigns, our ambitions do not always coincide with your priorities. We may be too concerned about the beauty of our place of worship and too little about the beauty of our lives and relationships with others. We need the mark of your grace upon us, your people, as well as a visible sanctuary for your worship. Forgive us if we are more jealous of the dignity of our name rather than yours. We pray in the name of Jesus. Amen.

• DECLARATION OF GOD'S FORGIVENESS
Hear the Good News! God's grace is all you need. Divine power comes to full strength in our weakness. Friends, believe the Good News! In Jesus Christ, we are forgiven.

• EXHORTATION
Prefer to find your joy and pride in the very things that are your weakness and then the power of Christ will come and rest upon you.

• PRAYER OF THE DAY
Penetrating Spirit, open our minds to the wisdom we may receive from hometown prophets. Touch our hearts with healing gifts that you have granted to our neighbors, so that your work may not be obstructed by our unbelief. Amen.

• PRAYER OF THANKSGIVING
God of surprises, you bring the wise to birth in unlikely places and skills of art and healing from families of unpromising histories. We are grateful for all wisdom expressed in speech, in writing, in music, in arts of all kinds. We appreciate healing words and touches that make us whole, especially the words of your Son, Jesus, and the comfort of your Holy Spirit. Amen.

- **PRAYER OF DEDICATION**

O God, bind together our gifts and ourselves by the Spirit in the church, that what otherwise would be weak may be strong and what otherwise would be insufficient may be sufficient to accomplish the mission of Christ in this place and in the whole world. Amen.

- **PSALM 48:1-14**

Great is the LORD
and greatly to be praised in the city of our God.
His holy mountain, beautiful in elevation, is the joy of all the earth,
Mount Zion, in the far north, the city of the great King.
Within its citadels God has shown himself a sure defense.
Then the kings assembled,
they came on together.
As soon as they saw it, they were astounded;
they were in panic, they took to flight;
trembling took hold of them there, pains as of a woman in labor,
as when an east wind shatters the ships of Tarshish.
As we have heard,
so have we seen in the city of the LORD of hosts,
in the city of our God, which God establishes forever.
We ponder your steadfast love, O God, in the midst of your temple.
Your name, O God, like your praise, reaches to the ends of the earth.
Your right hand is filled with victory.
Let Mount Zion be glad,
let the cities of Judah rejoice because of your judgments.
Walk about Zion, go all around it, count its towers,
consider well its ramparts; go through its citadels,
that you may tell the next generation that this is God,
our God forever and ever. He will be our guide forever.

PROPER 10

2 Samuel 6:1-5, 12b-19   Psalm 24
Ephesians 1:3-14   Mark 6:14-29

• CALL TO WORSHIP
Believers/Priests, you are clothed with the garments of salvation. Shout for joy, you loyal servants of the heavenly realm.

• PRAYER OF CONFESSION
How dangerous is the pride in which we attempt to compare our greatness to yours, O God! What lineage, however honorable, can be traced with confidence in your eternity? What national history or personal history, deserves to be mentioned in connection with the history of your saving acts? Forgive the haughtiness that accompanies our pride of race, or place, or person. Only by your grace are we received into the heavenly realms, through Jesus Christ our Savior. Amen.

• DECLARATION OF GOD'S FORGIVENESS
Hear the Good News! In Christ our release is secured and our sins are forgiven through the shedding of his blood. Friends, believe the Good News! In Jesus Christ, we are forgiven.

• EXHORTATION
Live for the praise of God's glory.

• PRAYER OF THE DAY
Lord of all being, we would offer all our artistic gifts to you rather than to any human authority, giving praise to you for all the beauty of creation by our own creativity however modest in comparison to yours; through Jesus Christ our redeemer. Amen.

• PRAYER OF THANKSGIVING
Parenting God, Adopter of children, Unifying Spirit, how can we evaluate the richness of your grace lavished on us in Jesus Christ? How can we estimate the treasure of wisdom and insight that you have graciously given us, disclosing the long-hidden purposes of your intention to unify all things in the universe in our Lord Jesus Christ? We can only praise you to the limits of our vocabulary. We can adore you to the full capacity of our loving. We can dedicate our lives to you in daily obedience to your direction. All glory be given to you, O God. Amen.

- **PRAYER OF DEDICATION**
Purposeful God, you honor us by including us in your plans for the universe. Receive our offerings and our promised willingness to fit into the place you have for us in the completion of your grand design in Jesus Christ. Amen.

- **PSALM 24:1-10**
The earth is the LORD's and all that is in it,
the world, and those who live in it;
for he has founded it on the seas,
and established it on the rivers.
Who shall ascend the hill of the LORD?
And who shall stand in his holy place?
Those who have clean hands and pure hearts,
who do not lift up their souls to what is false, and do not swear deceitfully.
They will receive blessing from the LORD,
and vindication from the God of their salvation.
Such is the company of those who seek him,
who seek the face of the God of Jacob.
Lift up your heads, O gates!
and be lifted up, O ancient doors!
that the King of glory may come in.
Who is the King of glory?
The LORD, strong and mighty,
the LORD, mighty in battle.
Lift up your heads, O gates!
and be lifted up, O ancient doors!
that the King of glory may come in.
Who is this King of glory?
The LORD of hosts,
he is the King of glory.

PROPER 11

2 Samuel 7:1-14a
Ephesians 2:11-22

Psalm 89:20-37
Mark 6:30-34, 53-56

- **CALL TO WORSHIP**

Relax. You have heard the invitation of the Christ to come to this quiet place for rest and renewal.

- **PRAYER OF CONFESSION**

Divine Shepherd, you seek to gather your scattered flock and bring them back to the way of righteousness. We are sorry for whatever we have done or failed to do that has estranged others from you rather than entreating them to come back to your fold. Forgive our own wandering and ungodly actions through Jesus Christ, who laid down his life as our Good Shepherd. Amen.

- **DECLARATION OF GOD'S FORGIVENESS**

Hear the Good News! Christ proclaims peace to you who were far off and now are made near by the blood of his cross. Friends, believe the Good News! In Jesus Christ, we are forgiven.

- **EXHORTATION**

Share the concern of Christ for his flock, that none may be without a shepherd.

- **PRAYER OF THE DAY**

Prince and Preacher of Peace, guide us in your ways and so inspire our words and actions by your Spirit that we may make gates where there are still walls between nations and nationalities, between churches and religions, all brought nearer to our eternal Parent. Amen.

- **PRAYER OF THANKSGIVING**

From what diversity of humanity you build your church, Divine Builder! With what grace you inhabit this temple making it holy by your presence within this human dwelling! We celebrate our foundation on apostles and prophets and especially the keystone, Jesus Christ! His cross mounted on the highest steeple can not do justice to the miracle of reconciliation accomplished by your covenant mercies. We exalt your name, One God, Architect, Builder, Inhabiting Spirit. Amen.

• **PRAYER OF DEDICATION**
You fulfill all our needs, O God, except our need to give to others and to you. Receive our offerings for the sake of your self-giving Son, Jesus Christ. Amen.

• **PSALM 89:20-37**
I have found my servant David;
with my holy oil I have anointed him;
my hand shall always remain with him;
my arm also shall strengthen him.
The enemy shall not outwit him,
the wicked shall not humble him.
I will crush his foes before him
and strike down those who hate him.
My faithfulness and steadfast love shall be with him;
and in my name his horn shall be exalted.
I will set his hand on the sea
and his right hand on the rivers.
He shall cry to me, "You are my Father,
my God, and the Rock of my salvation!"
I will make him the firstborn,
the highest of the kings of the earth.
Forever I will keep my steadfast love for him,
and my covenant with him will stand firm.
I will establish his line forever,
and his throne as long as the heavens endure.
If his children forsake my law and do not walk according to my ordinances,
if they violate my statutes and do not keep my commandments,
then I will punish their transgression with the rod and their iniquity with scourges;
but I will not remove from him my steadfast love, or be false to my faithfulness
I will not violate my covenant, or alter the word that went forth from my lips.
Once and for all I have sworn by my holiness; I will not lie to David.
His line shall continue forever,
and his throne endure before me like the sun.
It shall be established forever like the moon,
an enduring witness in the skies.

PROPER 12

2 Samuel 11:1-15　　　　　　　　　　　　　　　Psalm 14
Ephesians 3:14-21　　　　　　　　　　　　　　John 6:1-21

• CALL TO WORSHIP
Come without concealment to confess your sins. Return to your homes happy that your sins have been put away!

• PRAYER OF CONFESSION
God of nations, Sovereign of sovereigns, Protector of people, we do not understand why the innocent suffer for the sins of the guilty and the weak for the faults of the strong. We are strong in our denunciation of the sins of others and loud in our demands for their punishment. We are apologetic in the admission of our own sins and plaintive in our cries for mercy. Forgive our double standards, and grant us pardon for our offenses through Jesus our advocate. Amen.

• DECLARATION OF GOD'S FORGIVENESS
Hear the Good News! God has laid on the crucified Christ the consequences of our sins, so that we will not die. Friends, believe the Good News! In Jesus Christ, we are forgiven.

• EXHORTATION
Grasp what is the breadth and length and height and depth of the love of Christ, and to know it, though it is beyond knowledge. So may you attain to fullness of being, the fullness of God.

• PRAYER OF THE DAY
Modest Master, teach us to withdraw from the praise that would put us in the power of others and prevent our doing what you want us to do and when. Amen.

• PRAYER OF THANKSGIVING
God of all families in heaven and earth, receive our praise and thanksgiving for the manifestation of your love for us all in Jesus Christ. You do for us immeasurably more than we can ask or think. Your Spirit enriches our lives with a sense of your presence within us as well as around us and empowers our common service in the church of your dear Son. In generation after generation you inspire faith in Christ and regenerate your people. For all that you do, we give thanks. For all that you a are, we give praise, endlessly. Amen.

- **PRAYER OF DEDICATION**

Generous God, show us again what miracles you can do when we offer to you all that we have and all that we are, no matter how insignificant it may seem, through Jesus Christ our Lord. Amen.

- **PSALM 14:1-7**

Fools say in their hearts, "There is no God."
They are corrupt, they do abominable deeds;
there is no one who does good.
The LORD looks down from heaven on humankind
to see if there are any who are wise, who seek after God.
They have all gone astray, they are all alike perverse;
there is no one who does good, no, not one.
Have they no knowledge, all the evildoers who eat up my
people as they eat bread, and do not call upon the LORD?
There they shall be in great terror,
for God is with the company of the righteous.
You would confound the plans of the poor,
but the LORD is their refuge.
O that deliverance for Israel would come from Zion!
When the LORD restores the fortunes of his people,
Jacob will rejoice;
Israel will be glad.

PROPER 13

2 Samuel 11:26 - 12:13a
Ephesians 4:1-16

Psalm 51:1-12
John 6:24-35

- **CALL TO WORSHIP**

Come into God's presence with a clean heart, with a new and right spirit, indeed in the discipline of the Holy Spirit from me.

- **PRAYER OF CONFESSION**

Giver of manna, Breaker of bread, Creator of the new, it is true that we still do what we have not learned from Christ. We can be hardhearted when we should be forgiving. We can be selfish when we should be willing to share. We can be greedy and complaining when we have enough to get by. We can be as unscrupulous in our dealing as if we did not know what is just and true. Forgive us and finish your new creation through Jesus Christ. Amen.

- **DECLARATION OF GOD'S FORGIVENESS**

Hear the Good News! Hope is held out in God's call to you, one Christ, one faith, one baptism, one God, parent of us all. Friends, believe the Good News! In Jesus Christ, we are forgiven.

- **EXHORTATION**

Be humble always, and gentle, and patient too. Be forbearing with one another and charitable.

- **PRAYER OF THE DAY**

Giver of good things, Gift of God, Spirit of the self-giver, give us an appetite for the eternal life that we may not be satisfied with what perishes but devote our lives to the pursuit of spiritual excellence. Amen.

- **PRAYER OF THANKSGIVING**

Giver of all patience, Child of our humanity, renewing Spirit, we turn from our complaints about what we do not have to thanksgiving for the many good things you have given us. In addition to the simple nutrition of good bread and butter you give us the bread of angels, sustenance of the Spirit, the bread of life. We rejoice in the ideas and revelation that stimulate our thinking. We revel in the new joys that we experience in the shared intimacy of others with similar commitments to the truth. We are grateful for your patience in teaching us, your understanding through incarnational experience, your perseverance in developing our relationships. All praise to you perfect Parent, loving Brother, family Spirit. Amen.

- **PRAYER OF DEDICATION**
Generous Giver, we would emulate your generosity, making possible the sharing of bread of life at the Lord's table, and in the gathering of your people where they live and work and play, everywhere. Amen.

- **PSALM 51:1-12**
Have mercy on me, O God, according to your steadfast love;
according to your abundant mercy blot out my transgressions.
Wash me thoroughly from my iniquity,
and cleanse me from my sin.
For I know my transgressions,
and my sin is ever before me.
Against you, you alone, have I sinned,
and done what is evil in your sight,
so that you are justified in your sentence
and blameless when you pass judgment.
Indeed, I was born guilty,
a sinner when my mother conceived me.
You desire truth in the inward being;
therefore teach me wisdom in my secret heart.
Purge me with hyssop, and I shall be clean;
wash me, and I shall be whiter than snow.
Let me hear joy and gladness;
let the bones that you have crushed rejoice.
Hide your face from my sins,
and blot out all my iniquities.
Create in me a clean heart, O God,
and put a new and right spirit within me.
Do not cast me away from your presence,
and do not take your holy spirit from me.
Restore to me the joy of your salvation,
and sustain in me a willing spirit.

PROPER 14

2 Samuel 18:5-9, 15, 31-33   Psalm 130
Ephesians 4:25-5:2   John 6:35, 41-51

- **CALL TO WORSHIP**

Await God's presence and hope in God's word as if you were looking for the first light of dawn after a dark night.

- **PRAYER OF CONFESSION**

Loving and forgiving Parent, Loving and forgiving Christ, Loving and forgiving Spirit, we confess that we are not always generous, tenderhearted and forgiving. We can be spiteful in our behavior because of the bad feeling that we cherish in our hearts. That anger can come out in angry shouting and cursing which is not only offensive to others but grieves your Spirit within us. Forgive us for resisting the Spirit who is at work in us to make us more like Jesus Christ. Amen.

- **DECLARATION OF GOD'S FORGIVENESS**

Hear the Good News! God in Christ has forgiven you. Christ gave himself on your behalf as an offering and sacrifice whose fragrance is pleasing to God. Friends, believe the Good News! In Jesus Christ, we are forgiven.

- **EXHORTATION**

Be generous to one another, tender-hearted, forgiving one another as God in Christ forgave you.

- **PRAYER OF THE DAY**

Foster Son of Joseph, very Son of God, so teach us your way of self-giving that we may give ourselves in the service of others as you have given yourself for the life of the world. Amen.

- **PRAYER OF THANKSGIVING**

God of meadow and wilderness, Christ of human experience, Spirit of renewal and rest, we are thankful for the angel you send to minister to us. When we are depressed and ready to die, you send someone with a word of encouragement, or a gift of food or flowers or an invitation that leads to a change of scene and an opportunity to recover and go on. When our chins are on our chests, you send someone with a loving touch to raise our eyes to you. Joy and thanksgiving break through the clouds like the sun after a storm. We exalt your name together, everloving Parent, understanding Brother, Holy Spirit of God, eternal and liberating. Amen.

- **PRAYER OF DEDICATION**

As God's dear children, we come to you, trying to be like Jesus Christ, who loved you and gave himself up on our behalf as an offering and sacrifice whose fragrance is pleasing to you. Receive what we give of ourselves and of our name in the name of Jesus Christ. Amen.

- **PSALM 130:1-8**

Out of the depths I cry to you, O LORD. Lord, hear my voice!
Let your ears be attentive to the voice of my supplications!
If you, O LORD, should mark iniquities, Lord, who could stand?
But there is forgiveness with you, so that you may be revered.
I wait for the LORD,
my soul waits, and in his word I hope;
my soul waits for the Lord more than those who watch for the morning,
more than those who watch for the morning.
O Israel, hope in the LORD!
For with the LORD there is steadfast love,
and with him is great power to redeem.
It is he who will redeem Israel from all its iniquities.

PROPER 15

1 Kings 2:10-12; 3:3-14 Psalm 111
Ephesians 5:15-20 John 6:51-58

• CALL TO WORSHIP
Praise the LORD! Give thanks to the LORD with all your heart.

• PRAYER OF CONFESSION
Wise God, forgive our foolish preoccupation with things that don't matter. We are reluctant to open our minds to new ideas and broader views. We are content to love you with less than all our minds. We resist the discipline of study and sharing and self-evaluation that could help us to grow in wisdom like your Son, Jesus Christ. Amen.

• DECLARATION OF GOD'S FORGIVENESS
Hear the Good News! Jesus said, "As the living Father sent me, and I live because of the Father, so he who eats me shall live because of me." Friends, believe the Good News! In Jesus, Christ, we are forgiven.

• EXHORTATION
Be most careful how you conduct yourselves: like sensible people, not thoughtlessly. Use the present opportunity to the full, for these are evil days.

• PRAYER OF THE DAY
Whet our appetite, Giver of life, for the bread of life, Jesus Christ, that through our faith in him and our reception of him we may have life eternal, living with him day by day and raised by him on the last day. Amen.

• PRAYER OF THANKSGIVING
Founder of the feast, we give thanks today and every day for daily bread to sustain our bodies and the bread of life to restore our souls. We speak to one another in psalms and sing songs and hymns in praise of your goodness in the name of our Lord Jesus Christ. In silent times we make music in our hearts, full of joy, full of the Holy Spirit. For all who write words that we can say or sing we express our gratitude. For all who compose melodies that give zest to our celebration of your grace, we speak our praise. All praise to you, God of wisdom, beauty and truth. Amen.

- **PRAYER OF DEDICATION**
Creator and giver of all good things, we bring our offering of thanksgiving and declare our intentions to turn from evil and do good, to seek peace and pursue it. Teach us how to revere your name more fully through Jesus Christ our Lord. Amen.

- **PSALM 111:1-10**
Praise the LORD!
I will give thanks to the LORD with my whole heart,
in the company of the upright,
in the congregation.
Great are the works of the LORD,
studied by all who delight in them.
Full of honor and majesty is his work,
and his righteousness endures forever.
He has gained renown by his wonderful deeds;
the LORD is gracious and merciful.
He provides food for those who fear him;
he is ever mindful of his covenant.
He has shown his people the power of his works,
in giving them the heritage of the nations.
The works of his hands are faithful and just;
all his precepts are trustworthy.
They are established forever and ever,
to be performed with faithfulness and uprightness.
He sent redemption to his people;
he has commanded his covenant forever.
Holy and awesome is his name.
The fear of the LORD is the beginning of wisdom;
all those who practice it have a good understanding.
His praise endures forever.

PROPER 16

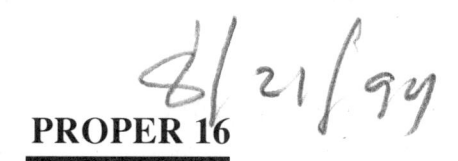

8/21/94

1 Kings 8:(1, 6, 10-11), 22-30, 41-43   Psalm 84
Ephesians 6:10-20   John 6:56-69

• CALL TO WORSHIP
Come to Christ whose words are words of eternal life. Have faith knowing that Jesus is the Holy One of God.

• PRAYER OF CONFESSION
God of the promise, you have declared yourself to be our heavenly Parent through Jesus Christ. Forgive our denial of your promised care through anxiety and our hesitancy to identify ourselves with you despite your past provision for our needs. We are sorry for the disloyalty we have shown you from time to time through our rejection of the church. Absolve us for the sake of your ever loyal Son, Jesus Christ. Amen.

• DECLARATION OF GOD'S FORGIVENESS
Hear the Good News! Christ loved the church and gave himself for it, to consecrate it, cleansing it by water and word so that he might present the church to himself all glorious, with no stain or wrinkle or anything of the sort, but holy and without blemish. Friends, believe the Good News! In Jesus Christ, we are forgiven.

• EXHORTATION
As member of the church, be subject to Christ and husbands and wives be subject to one another out of reverence for Christ.

• PRAYER OF THE DAY
Faithful God, when others leave you and your word, help us to be true to your Son, Jesus, no matter how hard that choice is and how unpopular. Steady us in our resolve to serve you always and to seek no easier service through Jesus Christ our Lord. Amen.

• PRAYER OF THANKSGIVING
Loving God, we sing your praise and shout for joy at the thought of your unstinting generosity and unflagging help. You sustain us in physical, mental and spiritual life. You provide support for us in the life of the church, in the intimacy of marriage and the encouragement of friendship. You are gracious and good and we honor you, God of Israel, Ruler of the church, universal Spirit. Amen.

• PRAYER OF DEDICATION

Christ our Lord, Head of the church, receive what we offer as members of your body. As we serve you, coordinate our efforts so that nothing that should be done is left undone and all your purposes accomplished to the glory of your name. Amen.

• PSALM 84

How lovely is your dwelling place, O LORD of hosts!
My soul longs, indeed it faints for the courts of the LORD;
my heart and my flesh sing for joy to the living God.
Even the sparrow finds a home,
and the swallow a nest for herself,
where she may lay her young,
at your altars, O LORD of hosts, my King and my God.
Happy are those who live in your house,
ever singing your praise.
Happy are those whose strength is in you,
in whose heart are the highways to Zion.
As they go through the valley of Baca they make it a place of springs;
the early rain also covers it with pools.
They go from strength to strength;
the God of gods will be seen in Zion.
O LORD God of hosts, hear my prayer;
give ear, O God of Jacob!
Behold our shield, O God;
look on the face of your anointed.
For a day in your courts is better than a thousand elsewhere.
I would rather be a doorkeeper in the house of my God than live in the tents of wickedness.
For the LORD God is a sun and shield;
he bestows favor and honor.
No good thing does the LORD withhold from those who walk uprightly.
O LORD of hosts, happy is everyone who trusts in you.

Proper 17

Song of Solomon 2:8-13　　　　　　　　　　Psalm 45:1-2, 6-9
James 1:17-27　　　　　　　　　　　　Mark 7:1-8, 14-15, 21-23

- **CALL TO WORSHIP**
Give yourselves wholly to prayer . . . always interceding for all God's people, and pray for me that I may be granted the right words to make known God's purpose.

- **PRAYER OF CONFESSION**
God above us, God around us, God within us, help us to distinguish between your law and the traditions of our society. We are prone to make decisions on opinions that everyone is doing it or that polls show us that we have a lot of company. Even though you have listed a horrendous catalogue of sins that come from within us, we have neglected our inner life. Save us from all our sins, divine Redeemer. Amen.

- **DECLARATION OF GOD'S FORGIVENESS**
Hear the Good News! The Spirit will give us inner strength to resist all evil. Friends, believe the Good News! In Jesus Christ, we are forgiven.

- **EXHORTATION**
Find your strength in the power of the Spirit so that you may be able to stand firm against all the devices of the devil.

- **PRAYER OF THE DAY**
Sovereign Spirit, so order our thoughts that our actions may give evidence of your inner rule in our lives and our worship be no vain lip-service but heartfelt obedience to your commands. Amen.

- **PRAYER OF THANKSGIVING**
God our guardian, we give hearty thanks that you do not leave us defenseless against the evil around us or already within us. Not only our physical safety but our spiritual security are of concern to you. We appreciate the many resources you have given us to fight against the ploys of the evil one. We enjoy the community of faith that supports us in our striving against sin. We rejoice in the victory of Christ over sin and death and will celebrate that conquest in eternity. Amen.

- **PRAYER OF DEDICATION**

Divine Commander, with all your people we would stand firm in support of your cause and in opposition to the dark forces of heaven and earth. Receive this pledge and these tokens of our allegiance. Amen.

- **PSALM 45:1-2, 6-9** A love song.

My heart overflows with a goodly theme;
I address my verses to the king;
my tongue is like the pen of a ready scribe.
You are the most handsome of men;
grace is poured upon your lips;
therefore God has blessed you forever.
Your throne, O God, endures forever and ever.
Your royal scepter is a scepter of equity;
you love righteousness and hate wickedness.
Therefore God, your God, has anointed you with the oil of gladness beyond your companions;
your robes are all fragrant with myrrh and aloes and cassia.
From ivory palaces stringed instruments make you glad;
daughters of kings are among your ladies of honor;
at your right hand stands the queen in gold of Ophir.

PROPER 18

Proverbs 22:1-2, 8-9, 22-23 Psalm 125
James 2:1-10, (11-13), 14-17 Mark 7:24-37

• **CALL TO WORSHIP**
Praise the Lord as long as you live. Sing psalms to God all your life long.

• **PRAYER OF CONFESSION**
Just God, you are even-handed in your justice and in the day of judgment will not play favorites. We confess that we are not so fair in our dealings. We are often unduly impressed by the powerful and the clever and excuse in them what we would condemn in the powerless and ignorant. Forgive superficiality and neglect of people needing advocacy and friendship, through the friend of sinners, Jesus Christ. Amen.

• **DECLARATION OF GOD'S FORGIVENESS**
Hear the Good News! God has chosen those who are poor in the eyes of the world to be rich in faith and to inherit the kingdom he has promised to those who love him. Friends, believe the Good News. In Jesus Christ, we are forgiven.

• **EXHORTATION**
Never show snobbery, believing as you do in our Lord Jesus Christ who reigns in glory.

• **PRAYER OF THE DAY**
Divine Physician, heal our hardness of hearing and soften our feelings so that we have your sensitivity to and awareness of the needs of others, often hidden behind a curtain of words. Free our tongues to share our innermost feeling with a trusted friend or counselor. Make us well, Jesus. Amen.

• **PRAYER OF THANKSGIVING**
We praise you, God of Israel, God of the church universal. You made the heavens and the earth, the sparrow and the gull, the whale and the minnow. You care for people, the hungry and the oppressed. You restore sight and help the stooped to stand tall. You give new heart to the bereaved and hopeless. Our hopes are in you and you will not disappoint us at the last. We praise you, Creator, Christ, Comforter. Amen.

- **PRAYER OF DEDICATION**

Divine Person, beyond all human personhood, transform these tangible but impersonal things into acts and gifts of persons-serving-persons in the name of Jesus Christ. Amen.

- **PSALM 125**

Those who trust in the LORD are like Mount Zion,
which cannot be moved, but abides forever.
As the mountains surround Jerusalem,
so the LORD surrounds his people,
from this time on and forevermore.
For the scepter of wickedness shall not rest on the land allotted to the righteous,
so that the righteous might not stretch out their hands to do wrong.
Do good, O LORD, to those who are good,
and to those who are upright in their hearts.
But those who turn aside to their own crooked ways
the LORD will lead away with evildoers.
Peace be upon Israel!

PROPER 19

Proverbs 1:20-33 Psalm 19 or Wisdom of Solomon 7:26-8:1
James 3:1-12 Mark 8:27-38

• CALL TO WORSHIP
Love the Lord, who has heard us and listens to our prayers. God has given us a hearing whenever we have cried out to heaven.

• PRAYER OF CONFESSION
Living and loving God, we worship you more readily in the presence of your friends, than in the company of your detractors. We don't find much blessedness in being persecuted and avoid confessing our faith rather than expose ourselves to ridicule or suffering. We do not have the courage of our convictions and play safe much of the time. Forgive our failure to live our supposed faith and to act on our declared sympathies through your long-suffering Son, Jesus Christ. Amen.

• DECLARATION OF GOD'S FORGIVENESS
Hear the Good News! Gracious is the Lord and righteous; our God is full of compassion. When we are brought low, God saves us. Friends, believe the Good News! In Jesus Christ, we are forgiven.

• EXHORTATION
Leave self behind, take up your cross and follow Jesus. Walk in the Lord's presence in the land of the living.

• PRAYER OF THE DAY
Suffering Savior, Son of the suffering God, grant us courage to accept suffering as well as healing and help for your name's sake. Give us inner strength in the Spirit to be faithful by the confession of your name, Jesus Christ, Son of the living God. Amen.

• PRAYER OF THANKSGIVING
God of life and health, we would thank you for health by caring for the sick. We should show our gratitude for freedom by working for the release of prisoners. We double our enjoyment of what we have by sharing with those who don't have. We echo the good news we have heard for those who live in the sadness of bad times. Receive the worship we present in word and deed in the Spirit of Jesus our Lord. Amen.

• PRAYER OF DEDICATION
Sovereign Lord, let our money talk for us in the hour of prayer, but also use it to send a word to the weary, to strengthen and to heal the sick in the name of Jesus. Amen.

• PSALM 19
The heavens are telling the glory of God;
and the firmament proclaims his handiwork.
Day to day pours forth speech,
and night to night declares knowledge.
There is no speech, nor are there words;
their voice is not heard;
yet their voice goes out through all the earth,
and their words to the end of the world.
In the heavens he has set a tent for the sun,
which comes out like a bridegroom from his wedding canopy,
and like a strong man runs its course with joy.
Its rising is from the end of the heavens,
and its circuit to the end of them;
and nothing is hid from its heat.
The law of the LORD is perfect, reviving the soul;
the decrees of the LORD are sure, making wise the simple;
the precepts of the LORD are right, rejoicing the heart;
the commandment of the LORD is clear, enlightening the eyes;
the fear of the LORD is pure, enduring forever;
the ordinances of the LORD are true and righteous altogether.
More to be desired are they than gold, even much fine gold;
sweeter also than honey, and drippings of the honeycomb.
Moreover by them is your servant warned;
in keeping them there is great reward.
But who can detect their errors?
Clear me from hidden faults.
Keep back your servant also from the insolent;
do not let them have dominion over me.
Then I shall be blameless,
and innocent of great transgression.
Let the words of my mouth and the meditation of my heart
be acceptable to you, O LORD, my rock and my redeemer.

(or)

• WISDOM 7:26 — 8:1

For she is a reflection of eternal light,
a spotless mirror of the working of God,
and an image of his goodness.
Although she is but one, she can do all things,
and while remaining in herself, she renews all things;
in every generation she passes into holy souls
and makes them friends of God, and prophets;
for God loves nothing so much as the person who lives with wisdom.
She is more beautiful than the sun,
and excels every constellation of the stars.
Compared with the light she is found to be superior,
for it is succeeded by the night,
but against wisdom evil does not prevail.
She reaches mightily from one end of the earth to the other,
and she orders all things well.

PROPER 20

Proverbs 31:10-31   Psalm 1
James 3:13-4:3, 7-8a   Mark 9:30-37

• CALL TO WORSHIP
Turn your thoughts to God who is your helper and who will be the mainstay of your life.

• PRAYER OF CONFESSION
God of the gospel, the One who sends, The One who is sent and returns, the One who is sent and remains with the church, we declare our need of the wisdom that is from above, pure, peace-loving, considerate, open to reason. We can be devious rather than straightforward, hypocritical rather than sincere, unforgiving rather than merciful, cruel rather than kind. Forgive the bitter jealousy that leads to quarreling, the selfish ambition that destroys those who are in the way, the ungoverned passions that lead to disorder and evil of every kind. Temper your justice with mercy for the sake of your obedient Son, Jesus our peacemaker. Amen.

• DECLARATION OF GOD'S FORGIVENESS
Hear the Good News! God comes to those who welcome even a child in the name of Jesus. Friends, believe the Good News. In Jesus Christ, we are forgiven.

• EXHORTATION
Show wisdom and understanding by deeds done in the humility that comes from wisdom.

• PRAYER OF THE DAY
Galilean Jesus, mortal human, living Christ, teach us the greatness that is expressed by the embrace of a child rather than by rubbing shoulders with the powerful so that we may serve in the manner of your servanthood. Amen.

• PRAYER OF THANKSGIVING
God of wisdom, you are generous in sharing your wisdom with all who are receptive. Loving God, your kindness is exemplified in the humanity of Jesus and his openness to children. Spirit of peace, you can pacify our aggressiveness with our enemies. We are grateful for all that you have done for us in the events of Good Friday, and Easter, and Pentecost. We appreciate the kindly deeds you have inspired to diminish the evils that still

abound in our sinful world. With thanksgiving for what you have enabled your people to reap from the seeds of peace, we look for the further harvest of peacemaking, true justice. All praise be given to you, O God. Amen.

• PRAYER OF DEDICATION
What we give to you, we give willingly in praise of your name for that is good. We have gathered to worship you, and we go out to serve you more humbly than before, with the help that you continue to give. Amen.

• PSALM 1
Happy are those who do not follow the advice of the wicked,
or take the path that sinners tread, or sit in the seat of scoffers;
but their delight is in the law of the LORD,
and on his law they meditate day and night.
They are like trees planted by streams of water,
which yield their fruit in its season,
and their leaves do not wither.
In all that they do, they prosper.
The wicked are not so,
but are like chaff that the wind drives away.
Therefore the wicked will not stand in the judgment,
nor sinners in the congregation of the righteous;
for the LORD watches over the way of the righteous,
but the way of the wicked will perish.

PROPER 21

Esther 7:1-6, 9-10; 9:20-22
James 5:13-20

Psalm 124
Mark 9:38-50

- **CALL TO WORSHIP**

Praise the name of the Lord, you servants of the Lord, who stand in the house of the Lord, in the temple courts of our God.

- **PRAYER OF CONFESSION**

Most powerful Judge, you hear the outcry of the powerless who are defrauded by the rich. You know without our telling you that we have frequently envied the wealthy even though we know that their possessions do not withstand death and decay. Forgive us if we have conspired with any to deny the rights of the poor or withheld from anyone the simplest help we were asked to give. You will, at the last set all things right, rewarding even the most humble service, as promised by Jesus our Messiah. Amen.

- **DECLARATION OF GOD'S FORGIVENESS**

Hear the Good News! The Lord will give his people justice and have compassion on his servants. Friends, believe the Good News. In Jesus Christ, we are forgiven.

- **EXHORTATION** *Charge*

Do not try to stop anyone who does work of divine power in the name of Jesus. Whoever is not against us is on our side.

- **PRAYER OF THE DAY**

Jesus, Messiah, Champion of God's rule, help us to gain control of our bodies so that we restrain all harmful actions and are free to serve others in modest ways that many may not notice but which will be rewarded by you, from whom nothing is hidden. Amen.

- **PRAYER OF THANKSGIVING**

We praise you, O God, for, though you do what you please, your pleasure is justice with compassion. We worship you, O God, for though you choose your servants as you wish, your elect people are called to serve all in obedience to you. We are awed by the powers of nature, but assured that there is no force or being that can overpower you. We are most grateful that you make yourself known to us through the healing and saving power of Jesus Christ, our Leader and Friend. Amen.

• PRAYER OF DEDICATION
Without the gifts of your Spirit, Generous God, we would be unable to worship you by word and by work, but you enable our service as we are obedient to the prompting of the Spirit through Jesus Christ our Lord. Amen.

• PSALM 124
If it had not been the LORD who was on our side —
let Israel now say —
if it had not been the LORD who was on our side,
when our enemies attacked us,
then they would have swallowed us up alive,
when their anger was kindled against us;
then the flood would have swept us away,
the torrent would have gone over us;
then over us would have gone the raging waters.
Blessed be the LORD,
who has not given us as prey to their teeth.
We have escaped like a bird from the snare of the fowlers;
the snare is broken, and we have escaped.
Our help is in the name of the LORD,
who made heaven and earth.

PROPER 22

Job 1:1, 2:1-10   Psalm 26
Hebrews 1:1-4; 2:5-12   Mark 10:2-16

- **CALL TO WORSHIP** (responsively)
Sing aloud a song of thanksgiving,
and tell all God's wondrous deeds.
Love the house in which we pray,
and the place where we give God glory.

- **PRAYER OF CONFESSION**
God unlimited, God self-limited, God extending our limits, surely you do not expect us to accept suffering without complaint! We are frustrated with illnesses that rage on, keeping us from doing the things that bring us satisfaction and recognition. Long nights and months of futility seem such a waste to us. Too often we question why it should happen to us, thinking ourselves to be better than others. We forget the exposure of your Son Jesus, to all the circumstances of our mortality. We ignore the spiritual growth that could be ours to prepare us to minister to other sufferers. Forgive our resistance to the healing of spirit and body that your Spirit can enable through our faith in Jesus Christ. Amen.

- **DECLARATION OF GOD'S FORGIVENESS**
Hear the Good News! In the Spirit Jesus still comes healing who suffer from various diseases and freeing many who are captives of evil. Friends, believe the Good News! In Jesus Christ, we are forgiven.

- **EXHORTATION**
Bear your part in spreading the Good News, whether in illness or health, weakness or strength, in the service of God.

- **PRAYER OF THE DAY**
Synagogue-preacher, sick-bed-visitor, exorcist-of-evil, so teach us, so heal us, so clear us of evil, that we may be ready learners and teachers, visitors of the sick and the shut-in, of other sinners, gathering around you in one needy company. Amen.

- **PRAYER OF THANKSGIVING**
Creator of stars, nurse to the wounded, healer of broken spirits: that you have power to rule the cosmos, fills us with awe. That you stoop to touch and heal us, fills us with amazement. You give new heart to the humble.

We thank you for all that sustains life, human, vegetable, animal. Receive the thanksgiving of all creation, the psalms of your people, the music of the birds, the sounds of all living things. Hear us wherever we gather to praise your name. Amen.

• **PRAYER OF DEDICATION**
God of the Gospel, we share the responsibility of spreading the Good News, with pastors and elders, evangelists and teachers, healers and nurses, identifying with all sorts and conditions of people in order to communicate the word of your grace in Jesus Christ. Amen.

• **PSALM 26:1-12**
Vindicate me, O LORD, for I have walked in my integrity,
and I have trusted in the LORD without wavering.
Prove me, O LORD, and try me;
test my heart and mind.
For your steadfast love is before my eyes,
and I walk in faithfulness to you.
I do not sit with the worthless,
nor do I consort with hypocrites;
I hate the company of evildoers,
and will not sit with the wicked.
I wash my hands in innocence,
and go around your altar, O LORD,
singing aloud a song of thanksgiving,
and telling all your wondrous deeds.
O LORD, I love the house in which you dwell,
and the place where your glory abides.
Do not sweep me away with sinners,
nor my life with the bloodthirsty,
those in whose hands are evil devices,
and whose right hands are full of bribes.
But as for me, I walk in my integrity;
redeem me, and be gracious to me.
My foot stands on level ground;
in the great congregation I will bless the LORD.

PROPER 23

Job 23:1-9, 16-17 Psalm 22:1-15
Hebrews 4:12-16 Mark 10:17-31

• **CALL TO WORSHIP**
Be satisfied with God's love when morning breaks and sing for joy and be glad all your days.

• **PRAYER OF CONFESSION**
God of all possibilities, Gatekeeper of heaven, Assayer of Eternal values, you only are good. It is simpler to recite your commandments than to do them. Even if we do them, we often neglect the poor and risk eternal human values for the sake of perishable riches. Take from us all encumbrances that would prevent our entering the place of your rule. Apart from you, our salvation is impossible. Through Jesus, our high priest we come expecting mercy and grace and timely help. Amen.

• **DECLARATION OF GOD'S FORGIVENESS**
Hear the Good News! Jesus is our high priest, able to sympathize with us in our weakness, because he has been tested in every way like we are, but without sin. He intercedes for us at the throne of our gracious God. Friends, believe the Good News! In Jesus Christ, we are forgiven.

• **EXHORTATION**
Seek your happiness in the pursuit of wisdom and the acquiring of understanding. Wisdom is more profitable than silver and that gain is better than gold.

• **PRAYER OF THE DAY**
Life's Gamemaster; we cannot hurdle all the expectations you have of us in order to win eternal life, so forgive our infractions of the rules and bring us to final victory with your needed help. Amen.

• **PRAYER OF THANKSGIVING**
God before all ages, God with all generations, God of the years to come, we are humbled by the thought of your eternal being. Your majesty inspires our praise. Your love moves us to sing and rejoice. The help of all good and delightful things sustains us in days of suffering. We trust you to lead us through the gate of wisdom, knowing that we can learn in days of suffering and gladness and years of testing and accomplishment. We will sing and be glad all our days, God of yesterday, today and tomorrow. Amen.

- **PRAYER OF DEDICATION**

All-seeing and all-knowing God, we cannot hide our thoughts and purposes from you. Sift the motives in our worship and stewardship so that we may worship you more truly, through Jesus Christ our High Priest. Amen.

- **PSALM 22:1-15**

My God, my God, why have you forsaken me?
Why are you so far from helping me,
from the words of my groaning?
O my God, I cry by day, but you do not answer;
and by night, but find no rest.
Yet you are holy,
enthroned on the praises of Israel.
In you our ancestors trusted;
they trusted, and you delivered them.
To you they cried, and were saved;
in you they trusted, and were not put to shame.
But I am a worm, and not human;
scorned by others, and despised by the people.
All who see me mock at me;
they make mouths at me, they shake their heads;
"Commit your cause to the LORD; let him deliver —
let him rescue the one in whom he delights!"
Yet it was you who took me from the womb;
you kept me safe on my mother's breast.
On you I was cast from my birth,
and since my mother bore me you have been my God.
Do not be far from me,
for trouble is near and there is no one to help.
Many bulls encircle me,
strong bulls of Bashan surround me;
they open wide their mouths at me,
like a ravening and roaring lion.
I am poured out like water,
and all my bones are out of joint;
my heart is like wax;
it is melted within my breast;
my mouth is dried up like a potsherd,
and my tongue sticks to my jaws;
you lay me in the dust of death.

PROPER 24

Job 38:1-7, (34-41) Psalm 104:1-9, 24, 35c
Hebrews 5:1-10 Mark 10:35-45

• CALL TO WORSHIP
Set your love on God who answers when you call for help in the time of trouble. Enjoy the fullness of salvation by the Most High.

• PRAYER OF CONFESSION
God of all life, we confess that we desire your will for us to be pleasure and prosperity. We have great difficulty accepting suffering as anything but evil, and we reject it as if it were beyond your power to redeem. Forgive our doubts and our unwillingness to serve you and others to the point of pain. In this we are unlike your Son and Mary's, Jesus Christ, who suffered with us and for us. Amen.

• DECLARATION OF GOD'S FORGIVENESS
Hear the Good News! Jesus Christ was named high priest by God and being perfected in the school of suffering is the source of eternal salvation for all who obey him. Friends, believe the Good News! In Jesus Christ, we are forgiven.

• EXHORTATION
Seek true greatness through serving, not waiting to be served, but serving each other and all within your reach.

• PRAYER OF THE DAY
Jesus Christ, Person for others, grant us a portion of your Spirit that we may willingly serve others, whether we are honored or ignored, understood or rejected, loved or despised. We cannot accept the cup of suffering or the baptism of pain without your very present help. Amen.

• PRAYER OF THANKSGIVING
Active Listener, Self-offering Priest, Spirit of Prayer, we offer you our thanksgiving for the eternal salvation that is ours through obedience of faith in Christ, named our High Priest forever. We are grateful for your patience with our ignorance and error and weakness understood so well by Jesus who gave up his life as a ransom for many. May our willingness to serve rather than be served, be a further expression of our gratitude, Most High, Most Humble, Most Loving God. Amen.

- **PRAYER OF DEDICATION**

Gracious God, if we have not received grace to give until it hurts, grant us the generosity to serve until it helps, so that you may be praised for our servanthood in the name of Jesus Christ. Amen.

- **PSALM 104:1-9, 24, 35c**

Bless the LORD, O my soul.
O LORD my God, you are very great.
You are clothed with honor and majesty,
wrapped in light as with a garment.
You stretch out the heavens like a tent,
you set the beams of your chambers on the waters,
you make the clouds your chariot,
you ride on the wings of the wind,
you make the winds your messengers,
fire and flame your ministers.
You set the earth on its foundations,
so that it shall never be shaken.
You cover it with the deep as with a garment;
the waters stood above the mountains.
At your rebuke they flee;
at the sound of your thunder they take to flight.
They rose up to the mountains,
ran down to the valleys to the place that you appointed for them.
You set a boundary that they may not pass,
so that they might not again cover the earth.
O LORD, how manifold are your works!
In wisdom you have made them all;
the earth is full of your creatures.
Bless the LORD, O my soul.
Praise the LORD!

PROPER 25

Job 42:1-6, 10-17
Hebrews 7:23-28

Psalm 34:1-8, (19-22)
Mark 10:46-52

- **CALL TO WORSHIP**
Rejoice and sing aloud for joy. The Lord has done great things for us.

- **PRAYER OF CONFESSION**
Observant Parent, you know who we are. We can be moved by the sight of hunger without stopping our waste of food. We see the limitations of some of our energy sources but are slow to change our ways of using more than we need. We observe hazards and hurts in confrontation and conflict but are unwilling to learn the arts of conciliation. For our intransigence and intractability through your strong but docile Son, Jesus of Nazareth. Amen.

- **DECLARATION OF GOD'S FORGIVENESS**
Hear the Good News! God has received Jesus Christ as our representative bearing gifts and sacrifices for our sins. Friends, believe the Good News! In Jesus Christ, we are forgiven.

- **EXHORTATION**
Follow the priestly example of Jesus Christ and bear patiently with the ignorant and the erring.

- **PRAYER OF THE DAY**
So that we may fittingly be called Christian, Divine Sightgiver, grant us the vision to see where you go before us on life's road that we may follow you more closely and serve others with your insights. Amen.

- **PRAYER OF THANKSGIVING**
You are more than fair, Good Lord, You are merciful. You are not stingy but magnanimous in your gifts of nature and grace. You are more than approachable: you are loving and outgoing. You are near us and with us and in all of your people everywhere. We do not love you enough but we do love you, Person condescending, Person incoming, and may yet love you more. Amen.

- **PRAYER OF DEDICATION**
Creator of Eden and paradise, plant in us the fruits of unselfishness after weeding out greed, through the living, giving spirit of Jesus. Amen.

• **PSALM 34:1-8, (19-22)**
I will bless the LORD at all times;
his praise shall continually be in my mouth.
My soul makes its boast in the LORD;
let the humble hear and be glad.
O magnify the LORD with me,
and let us exalt his name together.
I sought the LORD, and he answered me,
and delivered me from all my fears.
Look to him, and be radiant;
so your faces shall never be ashamed.
This poor soul cried, and was heard by the LORD,
and was saved from every trouble.
The angel of the LORD encamps around those who fear him,
and delivers them.
O taste and see that the LORD is good;
happy are those who take refuge in him.
(Many are the afflictions of the righteous,
but the LORD rescues them from them all.
He keeps all their bones;
not one of them will be broken.
Evil brings death to the wicked,
and those who hate the righteous will be condemned.
The LORD redeems the life of his servants;
none of those who take refuge in him will be condemned.)

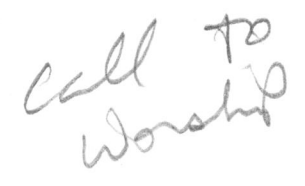

PROPER 26

Ruth 1:1-18   Psalm 146
Hebrews 9:11-14   Mark 12:28-34

• CALL TO WORSHIP
Praise the LORD as long as you live; sing praises to God all your life long.

• PRAYER OF CONFESSION
Good and great God, we come to you through Jesus Christ who intercedes for us sinners. We confess our sins seeking forgiveness not only that we may be at peace with you, but also that we may pray for others. We are ashamed that our prayers are often as self-centered as our lives. Excuse our disordered priorities as we seek to change and re-order our lives according to the teaching and spirit of Jesus Christ your Son, our Lord. Amen.

• DECLARATION OF GOD'S FORGIVENESS
Hear the Good News! God has chosen you to be saved through sanctification by the Spirit and belief in the truth. Friends, believe the Good News! In Jesus Christ, we are forgiven.

• EXHORTATION
To this he called you through the gospel, so that you may obtain the glory of our Lord Jesus Christ.

• PRAYER OF THE DAY
Integrate our lives, One God, in an all-embracing love of which you are the center and from whose encompassing Spirit none are excluded whether near or far, through Jesus Christ your loving-to-the-point-of-suffering Son. Amen.

• PRAYER OF THANKSGIVING
Who can number the bounties of your goodness, Lord? You give us lands overflowing with milk and honey and seas alive with fish and growing things. Our skies shine with beauty and with power. The depths of the earth yield metals and energy sources in great variety. Our homes are visited by friends, and our neighbors help us in times of need. We have opportunities to learn together, to worship together, and to serve the common good together. We worship you with thankful hearts, with open minds, with willing hands, in the Spirit of Jesus Christ. Amen.

- **PRAYER OF DEDICATION**

Lord, save us from hypocrisy, not serving you with these offerings only, and ourselves with what remains in our keeping. Help us to use all our energies and all our means to serve you and our neighbors as ourselves, through Jesus Christ our Lord. Amen.

- **PSALM 146:1-10**

Praise the LORD!
Praise the LORD, O my soul!
I will praise the LORD as long as I live;
I will sing praises to my God all my life long.
Do not put your trust in princes,
in mortals, in whom there is no help.
When their breath departs, they return to the earth;
on that very day their plans perish.
Happy are those whose help is the God of Jacob,
whose hope is in the LORD their God,
who made heaven and earth,
the sea, and all that is in them;
who keeps faith forever;
who executes justice for the oppressed;
who gives food to the hungry.
The LORD sets the prisoners free;
the LORD opens the eyes of the blind.
The LORD lifts up those who are bowed down;
the LORD loves the righteous.
The LORD watches over the strangers;
he upholds the orphan and the widow,
but the way of the wicked he brings to ruin.
The LORD will reign forever,
your God, O Zion, for all generations.
Praise the LORD!

PROPER 27

Ruth 3:1-5; 4:13-17
Hebrews 9:24-28

Psalm 127
Mark 12:38-44

- **CALL TO WORSHIP**

Come to worship in simplicity and sincerity. Vow to serve God in your daily life as you say your prayers in this company.

- **PRAYER OF CONFESSION**

Divine Provider, we confess that we sometimes doubt your provision for us. When we start scraping the bottom of the barrel, we cut back our sharing with others who have already run out and are hungry or in need. Forgive selfishness and independence that prevents interdependence and working together to solve distribution problems in the use of the resources of your good earth, through your compassionate Son, Jesus Christ. Amen.

- **DECLARATION OF GOD'S FORGIVENESS**

Hear the Good News! Christ has entered not into a sanctuary made with hands, a copy of the true one but into heaven itself now to appear in the presence of God on our behalf. Friends, believe the Good News! In Jesus Christ, we are forgiven.

- **EXHORTATION**

Just as it is appointed for us to die once and after that the judgment, so Christ having been offered once to bear the sins of many will appear a second time, not to deal with sin but to save those who are eagerly waiting for him. Encourage one another as you see the day drawing near.

- **PRAYER OF THE DAY**

Save us, good Lord, from half-heartedness in our service of your church. Help us to find joy in the full use of all that we are and have in the saving name of Jesus Christ of Nazareth. Amen.

- **PRAYER OF THANKSGIVING**

Creator, Redeemer, Renewer, we give thanks for the fruitfulness of our vineyards and orchards, the productivity of our fields, and the reproduction of our cattle and poultry. We praise your name for sunshine and rain. We will give thanks also by our work, reclaiming over-used lands, irrigating dry land, purifying polluted streams and lakes. We will be faithful managers of your lands and seas to the glory of your name and the benefit of generations still to be born. Amen.

• **PRAYER OF DEDICATION**
Holy God, what we give is nothing compared to the one-for-all, once-for-all sacrifice by Jesus of himself to put away our sins. Use our offering and witness to spread the good news of Jesus Christ, your Son and Savior of the world. Amen.

• **PSALM 127:1-5**
Unless the LORD builds the house,
those who build it labor in vain.
Unless the LORD guards the city,
the guard keeps watch in vain.
It is in vain that you rise up early and go late to rest,
eating the bread of anxious toil; for he gives sleep to his beloved.
Sons are indeed a heritage from the LORD,
the fruit of the womb a reward.
Like arrows in the hand of a warrior are the sons of one's youth.
Happy is the man who has his quiver full of them.
He shall not be put to shame when he speaks with his enemies in the gate.

PROPER 28

1 Samuel 1:4-20
Hebrews 10:11-14, (15-18)

1 Samuel 2:1-10
Mark 13:1-8

- **CALL TO WORSHIP**

Let us proclaim how mighty are the deeds of God, how glorious is the majesty of God's realm.

- **PRAYER OF CONFESSION**

Glorious God, Divine Human, Eternal Spirit, we get so mired in the stuff of every day that we rarely see visions and dream dreams. We are busy about daily routines for making a living and so preoccupied with the immediate that we do not look for signs of your judgment nor the changing seasons of divine history. Forgive our sins and wicked deeds for the sake of Christ's offering for our sins once and for all. Amen.

- **DECLARATION OF GOD'S FORGIVENESS**

Hear the Good News! Christ offered for all time one sacrifice for sins and took his seat at the right hand of God. Friends, believe the Good News! In Jesus Christ, we are forgiven.

- **EXHORTATION**

Be alert and wakeful, for you do not know when the head of the human household will return to take account of our stewardship of the earth.

- **PRAYER OF THE DAY**

Offspring of time and eternity, in monotonous times as well as in times of personal and communal crises, remind us of the limits of time so that the breaking in again of the eternal will not catch us unaware. Amen.

- **PRAYER OF THANKSGIVING**

Ancient in years, Offspring of time and eternity, timeless One, we are grateful for the moments in time when we are given a glimpse of eternity — when the poignancy of poetry or story give us full appreciation of love; when the coming together of people achieves fulfillment of true community; when a high moment of music or other living art gives us a vision of ageless beauty; when a prophetic word or action discloses the vision of truth. Be worshipped, O God, now and ever. Amen.

- **PRAYER OF DEDICATION**

True God, there are offerings for sin no longer for by the offering of Christ have all been consecrated. What we offer then is what is being perfected for all time by that climactic sacrifice of Jesus Christ. Amen.

- **1 SAMUEL 2:1-10**

Hannah prayed and said,
"My heart exults in the LORD;
my strength is exalted in my God.
My mouth derides my enemies,
because I rejoice in my victory.
"There is no Holy One like the LORD, no one besides you;
there is no Rock like our God.
Talk no more so very proudly,
let not arrogance come from your mouth;
for the LORD is a God of knowledge,
and by him actions are weighed.
The bows of the mighty are broken,
but the feeble gird on strength.
Those who were full have hired themselves out for bread,
but those who were hungry are fat with spoil.
The barren has borne seven,
but she who has many children is forlorn.
The LORD kills and brings to life;
he brings down to Sheol and raises up.
The LORD makes poor and makes rich;
he brings low, he also exalts.
He raises up the poor from the dust;
he lifts the needy from the ash heap,
to make them sit with princes and inherit a seat of honor.
For the pillars of the earth are the LORD's,
and on them he has set the world.
"He will guard the feet of his faithful ones,
but the wicked shall be cut off in darkness;
for not by might does one prevail.
The LORD! His adversaries shall be shattered;
the Most High will thunder in heaven.
The LORD will judge the ends of the earth;
he will give strength to his king,
and exalt the power of his anointed."

CHRIST THE KING

2 Samuel 23:1-7　　　　　　　　　　Psalm 132:1-12, (13-18)
Revelation 1:4b-8　　　　　　　　　　　　　John 18:33-37

• CALL TO WORSHIP
Holiness is the beauty of God's temple while time shall last. Worship God in the sanctity and freedom from our sins which Christ gives us through his life's blood.

• PRAYER OF CONFESSION
Ancient in year, First-born from the dead, timeless Spirit, we confess that too often we are overawed by the wealth and power of human rulers forgetting that they are as mortal as we are, and that only Jesus Christ has won an impressive victory over death. Forgive us if political and national loyalties have superseded the dignity you offer us as a royal house of priests to serve you. You have sent us your faithful Son Jesus Christ, but we listen to him less attentively than to less demanding voices around us. We admit that we too are among the people whose sins have wounded him. Forgive and free us from all our sins by the giving of his life's blood. Amen.

• DECLARATION OF GOD'S FORGIVENESS
Hear the Good News! The Christ loves us and frees us from our sins with his life's blood to make us a royal house to serve as priests of his God and Father. Friends, believe the Good News! In Jesus Christ, we are forgiven.

• EXHORTATION
Look for the one who is coming with the clouds! Call to repentance all who have offended him.

• PRAYER OF THE DAY
Sovereign of all, who is and who was, and who is to come, raise us above the tides of natural events, and the ebb and flow of history, so that we may glimpse the glory of your eternal realm, and be satisfied with no lesser honor than to serve you as witness to the truth in the company of Jesus Christ. Amen.

• PRAYER OF THANKSGIVING
Your majesty, eternal God, precedes and exceeds the grandeur of the seas, and your throne, unlike the passing dynasties of nations, does not pass away. Your truth, Sovereign over all earthly rulers, is full of grace and peace and not full of empty threatening so typical of the tyrants of our world. We join with the Seven Spirits before your throne in extolling you, the Alpha and the Omega, who is and who was and who is to come. May

our thanksgiving continue not only while we have life and breath, but through such coming generations as shall live until all people and nations of every language shall serve you. Amen.

- **PRAYER OF DEDICATION**
Our greatest gifts, Sovereign Creator, may not be given with pride, because none can be worthy of your majesty. Receive them as token tributes to you signifying our humble service in the royal priesthood of all believers, through Jesus Christ, our Princely Priest. Amen.

- **PSALM 132:1-12, (13-18)**
O LORD, remember in David's favor all the hardships he endured;
how he swore to the LORD and vowed to the Mighty One of Jacob,
"I will not enter my house or get into my bed;
I will not give sleep to my eyes or slumber to my eyelids,
until I find a place for the LORD,
a dwelling place for the Mighty One of Jacob."
We heard of it in Ephrathah;
we found it in the fields of Jaar.
"Let us go to his dwelling place;
let us worship at his footstool."
Rise up, O LORD, and go to your resting place,
you and the ark of your might.
Let your priests be clothed with righteousness,
and let your faithful shout for joy.
For your servant David's sake do not turn away the face
of your anointed one.
The LORD swore to David a sure oath from which he will
not turn back: "One of the sons of your body I will set on your throne.
(If your sons keep my covenant and my decrees that I shall teach them,
their sons also, forevermore, shall sit on your throne."
For the LORD has chosen Zion;
he has desired it for his habitation:
"This is my resting place forever;
here I will reside, for I have desired it.
I will abundantly bless its provisions;
I will satisfy its poor with bread.
Its priests I will clothe with salvation,
and its faithful will shout for joy.
There I will cause a horn to sprout up for David;
I have prepared a lamp for my anointed one.
His enemies I will clothe with disgrace,
but on him, his crown will gleam.")

145

ALL SAINTS'

Isaiah 25:6-9   Psalm 24
Revelation 21:1-6a   John 11:32-44

• CALL TO WORSHIP
God has spoken. Let us be glad and rejoice in the salvation of God.

• PRAYER OF CONFESSION
Eternal God, nothing is more awesome for us than the death which we know to be inevitable but which we can not fully understand. We often question the timeliness of death, wondering if it is really occasioned by your plan or only the result of natural causes. Forgive any doubts that we may have that the resurrection of Jesus Christ does not hold promise for us and all your people as well. In his name we pray. Amen.

• DECLARATION OF GOD'S FORGIVENESS
Hear the Good News! The faithful will abide with God in love, because grace and mercy are upon the holy ones of God who watches over the chosen in Christ. Friends, believe the Good News! In Jesus Christ, we are forgiven.

• EXHORTATION
Trust in God and you will understand all the truth you need on this side of the grave and have strong hope of eternity with God.

• PRAYER OF THE DAY
Jesus, Lord of life and death, free us from the fears that bind us and help us to live a day at a time trusting that you will provide for us what we need and in the end will take us to the place you have gone to prepare for us. Amen.

• PRAYER OF THANKSGIVING
God our savior, Christ our pioneer, Eternal Spirit, we give hearty thanks for our hopes of life everlasting. Your prophets foresee banquets and other signs of your abounding grace. Your word promises the intimacy of personal caring and the wiping away of the last of our tears. Who can fully imagine the glories prepared by the Risen Christ for those who will be received through his grace? All glory be given to you the Alpha and the Omega, the Beginning and the End, the Creator of life and our final Home. Amen.

- **PRAYER OF DEDICATION**

God invisible, God incarnate, God inspiring, the offerings we bring to our Lord's table are simple signs of our hope for the great feast you prepare in heaven. Receive these gifts and the offering of ourselves as living sacrifices acceptable to you through Jesus Christ our Lord. Amen.

- **PSALM 24:1-10**

The earth is the LORD's and all that is in it,
the world, and those who live in it;
for he has founded it on the seas,
and established it on the rivers.
Who shall ascend the hill of the LORD?
And who shall stand in his holy place?
Those who have clean hands and pure hearts,
who do not lift up their souls to what is false, and do not swear deceitfully.
They will receive blessing from the LORD,
and vindication from the God of their salvation.
Such is the company of those who seek him,
who seek the face of the God of Jacob.
Lift up your heads, O gates!
and be lifted up, O ancient doors! that the King of glory may come in.
Who is the King of glory?
The LORD, strong and mighty, the LORD, mighty in battle.
Lift up your heads, O gates!
and be lifted up, O ancient doors! that the King of glory may come in.
Who is this King of glory?
The LORD of hosts, he is the King of glory.

THANKSGIVING DAY

Joel 2:21-27　　　　　　　　　　　　　　　　　　Psalm 126
1 Timothy 2:1-7　　　　　　　　　　　　　　　Matthew 6:25-33

• CALL TO WORSHIP
You have eaten in plenty and been satisfied. Praise the name of God our creator and provider, who has dealt wondrously with us.

• PRAYER OF CONFESSION
Creator, Redeemer, and Sustainer of all life, we often complain about the weather wishing we were somewhere else where the weather was more to our liking. We fuss about food not entirely to our taste however nutritious. We are annoyed if we need medicine even if it improves our health and well being. Forgive our thanklessness and our anxieties when things run short. We need the Spirit of Jesus Christ. Amen.

• DECLARATION OF GOD'S FORGIVENESS
Hear the Good News! There is one God; there is also one mediator between God and humankind, Christ Jesus, himself human, who gave himself, a ransom for all. Friends, believe the Good News! In Jesus Christ, we are forgiven.

• EXHORTATION
Strive first for the dominion of God and the righteousness of God's realm, and all needful things will be given to you as well.

• PRAYER OF THE DAY
Heavenly Parent, make us mindful of the many provisions you make for your children in things temporal and things eternal that we may be content with what we have now, and eager for the perfections of eternity, through Jesus Christ our Lord. Amen.

• PRAYER OF THANKSGIVING
Great God, we give humble and hearty thanksgiving for the blessings of your creation; for the good earth and rich crops, for poultry and cattle and the harvest of the sea, for orchards and vineyards, for sunshine and rain, and the changing seasons. You generously give us wine to gladden the human heart, oil to make the face shine, and bread to strengthen the human heart. For good medicines to heal our bodies and for sacraments of your grace to heal and sustain our spirits we praise your name, God in creation, in Christ, in the Church. Amen.

- **PRAYER OF DEDICATION**

Without your creation there would be nothing for us to bring to you as tokens of our thanksgiving, O God. Receive what we offer in sincerity and humility, through Jesus Christ our Savior. Amen.

- **PSALM 126:1-6**

When the LORD restored the fortunes of Zion,
we were like those who dream.
Then our mouth was filled with laughter,
and our tongue with shouts of joy;
then it was said among the nations,
"The LORD has done great things for them."
The LORD has done great things for us, and we rejoiced.
Restore our fortunes, O LORD, like the watercourses in the Negeb.
May those who sow in tears reap with shouts of joy.
Those who go out weeping, bearing the seed for sowing, shall come home with shouts of joy, carrying their sheaves.

INDEX FOR SCRIPTURE PASSAGES

GENESIS
1:1-5 — EPIPHANY 1
9:8-17 — LENT 1
17:1-7, 15-16 — LENT 2

EXODUS
20:1-17 — LENT 3

NUMBERS
21:4-9 — LENT 4

DEUTERONOMY
5:12-15 — EPIPHANY 9
18:15-20 — EPIPHANY 4

RUTH
1:1-18 — PROPER 26
3:1-5; 4:13-17 — PROPER 27

FIRST SAMUEL
1:4-20 — PROPER 28
2:1-10 — PROPER 28
3:1-10, (11-20) — EPIPHANY 2
3:1-10, (11-20) — PROPER 4
8:4-11, (12-15), 16-20, (11:14-15) — PROPER 5
15:34 - 16:13 — PROPER 6
17:(1a,4-11,19-23) 32-49 — PROPER 7
(ALT) 17:57-18:5, 10-16 — PROPER 7

SECOND SAMUEL
1:1, 17-27 — PROPER 8
5:1-5, 9-10 — PROPER 9
6:1-5, 12b-19 — PROPER 10
7:1-11, 16 — ADVENT 4
7:1-14a — PROPER 11
11:1-15 — PROPER 12
11:26-12:13a — PROPER 13
18: 5-9, 15,31-33 — PROPER 14
23:1-7 — CHRIST THE KING

FIRST KINGS
2:10-12; 3:3-14 — PROPER 15
8:(1, 6, 10-11), 22-30, 41-43 — PROPER 16

SECOND KINGS
2:1-12 — TRANSFIGURATION
5:1-14 — EPIPHANY 6

ESTHER
7:1-6, 9-10; 9:20-22 — PROPER 21

JOB
1:1, 2:1-10 — PROPER 22
23:1-9, 16-17 — PROPER 23
38:1-7, (34-41) — PROPER 24
42:1-6, 10-17 — PROPER 25

PSALMS
1 — EASTER 7
1 — PROPER 20
4 — EASTER 3
8 — NEW YEARS EVE/DAY
9:9-20 — PROPER 7
14 — PROPER 12
19:1-14 — LENT 3
19 — PROPER 19
20 — PROPER 6
22:1-15 — PROPER 23
22:23-31 — LENT 2
22:25-31 — EASTER 5
23 — EASTER 4
24 — PROPER 10
24 — ALL SAINTS'
25:1-10 — LENT 1
26 — PROPER 22
29 — EPIPHANY 1
29 — TRINITY
30 — EPIPHANY 6
31:9-16 — LENT 6 Passion
34:1-8, (19-22) — PROPER 25
41 — EPIPHANY 7
45:1-2, 6-9 — PROPER 17
47 — ASCENSION DAY
48 — PROPER 9
50:1-6 — TRANSFIGURATION
51:1-12 — PROPER 13
51:1-12 — LENT 5
51:1-17 — ASH WEDNESDAY
62:5-12 — EPIPHANY 3
72:1-7, 10-14 — EPIPHANY
80:1-7, 17-19 — ADVENT 1
81:1-10 — EPIPHANY 9
84 — PROPER 16
85:1-2, 8-13 — ADVENT 2

150

89:1-4, 19-26	ADVENT 4	43:18-25	EPIPHANY 7
89:20-37	PROPER 11	50:4-9a	LENT 6 Passion
96	CHRISTMAS EVE/DAY (First)	50:4-9a	LENT 6 Palm
97	CHRISTMAS DAY (Second)	52:7-10	CHRISTMAS (THIRD)
98	CHRISTMAS (Third)	(ALT) 58:1-12	ASH WEDNESDAY
98	EASTER 6	60:1-6	EPIPHANY
103:1-13, 22	EPIPHANY 8	61:1-4, 8-11	ADVENT 3
104:1-9, 24, 35c	PROPER 24	61:10-62:3	CHRISTMAS 1
104: 24-34, 35b	PENTECOST	62:6-12	CHRISTMAS DAY (Second)
107:1-3, 17-22	LENT 4	64:1-9	ADVENT 1
111	PROPER 15		
111	EPIPHANY 4	**JEREMIAH**	
118:1-2,19-29	LENT 6 Palm	31:7-14	CHRISTMAS 2
118:1-2, 14-24	EASTER	31:31-34	LENT 5
119:9-16	LENT 5		
124	PROPER 21	**EZEKIEL**	
125	PROPER 18	(ALT) 37:1-14	PENTECOST
126	ADVENT 3		
126	THANKSGIVING	**HOSEA**	
127	PROPER 27	2:14-20	EPIPHANY 8
130	PROPER 14		
130	PROPER 8	**JOEL**	
132:1-12, (13-18)	CHRIST THE KING	2:1-2,12-17a	ASH WEDNESDAY
(ALT) 133	PROPER 7	2:21-27	THANKSGIVING
133	EASTER 2		
138	PROPER 5	**JONAH**	
139:1-6, 13-18	EPIPHANY 2	3:1-5,10	EPIPHANY 3
139:1-6, 13-18	PROPER 4		
146	PROPER 26	**WISDOM OF SIRACH**	
147:1-11, 20c	EPIPHANY 5	(ALT) 24:1-12	CHRISTMAS 2
147:12-20	CHRISTMAS 2		
148	CHRISTMAS 1	**WISDOM OF SOLOMON**	
		(ALT) 3:1-9	ALL SAINTS'
PROVERBS		(ALT) 7:26-8:1	PROPER 19
1:20-33	PROPER 19	(ALT) 10:15-21	CHRISTMAS 2
22:1-2, 8-9, 22-23	PROPER 18		
31:10-31	PROPER 20	**MATTHEW**	
		2:1-12	EPIPHANY
ECCLESIASTES		6:1-6, 16-21	ASH WEDNESDAY
3:1-13	NEW YEARS EVE/DAY	6:25-33	THANKSGIVING
		25:31-46	NEW YEARS EVE/DAY
SONG OF SOLOMON			
2:8-13	PROPER 17	**MARK**	
		1:1-8	ADVENT 2
ISAIAH		1:4-11	EPIPHANY 1
6:1-8	TRINITY	1:9-15	LENT 1
9:2-7	CHRISTMAS EVE/DAY (First)	1:14-20	EPIPHANY 3
25:6-9	ALL SAINTS	1:21-28	EPIPHANY 4
(ALT) 25:6-9	EASTER	1:29-39	EPIPHANY 5
40:1-11	ADVENT 2	1:40-45	EPIPHANY 6
40:21-31	EPIPHANY 5	2:1-12	EPIPHANY 7

2:18-22	EPIPHANY 8	6:51-58	PROPER 15
2:23-3:6	EPIPHANY 9	6:56-69	PROPER 16
2:23-3:6	PROPER 4	10:11-18	EASTER 4
3:20-35	PROPER 5	11:32-44	ALL SAINTS
4:26-34	PROPER 6	(ALT) 12:12-16	LENT 6 Palm
4:35-41	PROPER 7	12:20-33	LENT 5
5:21-43	PROPER 8	15:1-8	EASTER 5
6:1-13	PROPER 9	15:9-17	EASTER 6
6:14-29	PROPER 10	15:26-27; 16:4b-15	PENTECOST
6:30-34, 53-56	PROPER 11	17:6-19	EASTER 7
7:1-8,14-15,21-23	PROPER 17	18:33-37	CHRIST THE KING
7:24-37	PROPER 18	20:1-18	EASTER
8:27-38	PROPER 19	20:19-31	EASTER 2
8:31-38	LENT 2		
9:2-9	LENT 2	**ACTS**	
9:2-9	TRANSFIGURATION	1:1-11	ASCENSION DAY
9:30-37	PROPER 20	1:15-17,21-26	EASTER 7
10:2-16	PROPER 22	2:1-21	PENTECOST
10:17-31	PROPER 23	3:12-19	EASTER 3
10:35-45	PROPER 24	4:5-12	EASTER 4
10:46-52	PROPER 25	4:32-35	EASTER 2
11:1-11	LENT 6 Palm	8:26-40	EASTER 5
12:28-34	PROPER 26	10:34-43	EASTER
12:38-44	PROPER 27	10:44-48	EASTER 6
13:1-8	PROPER 28	19:1-7	EPIPHANY 1
13:24-37	ADVENT 1		
14:1-15:47	LENT 6 Passion	**ROMANS**	
(ALT) 15:1-39 (40-47)	LENT 6 Passion	4:13-25	LENT 2
(ALT) 16:1-8	EASTER	8:12-17	TRINITY
		8:22-27	PENTECOST
LUKE		16:25-27	ADVENT 4
1:26-38	ADVENT 4		
(ALT) 1:46b-55	ADVENT 3	**1 CORINTHIANS**	
1:47-55	ADVENT 4	1:3-9	ADVENT 1
2:1-14 (15-20)	CHRISTMAS EVE/DAY (First)	1:18-25	LENT 3
2:(1-7) 8-20	CHRISTMAS DAY (Second)	6:12-20	EPIPHANY 2
2:22-40	CHRISTMAS 1	7:29-31	EPIPHANY 3
24:36b-48	EASTER 3	8:1-13	EPIPHANY 4
24:44-53	ASCENSION DAY	9:16-23	EPIPHANY 5
		9:24-27	EPIPHANY 6
JOHN		15:1-11	EASTER
1:(1-9), 10-18	CHRISTMAS 2		
1:1-14	CHRISTMAS (THIRD)	**2 CORINTHIANS**	
1:6-8, 19-28	ADVENT 3	1:18-22	EPIPHANY 7
1:43-51	EPIPHANY 2	3:1-6	EPIPHANY 8
2:13-22	LENT 3	4:3-6	TRANSFIGURATION
3:1-17	TRINITY	4:5-12	PROPER 4
3:14-21	LENT 4	4:5-12	EPIPHANY 9
6:1-21	PROPER 12	4:13-5:1	PROPER 5
6:24-35	PROPER 13	5:6-10, (11-13), 14-17	PROPER 6
6:35, 41-51	PROPER 14	5:20b-6:10	ASH WEDNESDAY

6:1-13	PROPER 7
8:7-15	PROPER 8
12:2-10	PROPER 9

GALATIANS
4:4-7	CHRISTMAS 1

EPHESIANS
1:3-14	CHRISTMAS 2
1:3-14	PROPER 10
1:15-23	ASCENSION DAY
2:1-10	LENT 4
2:11-22	PROPER 11
3:1-12	EPIPHANY
3:14-21	PROPER 12
4:1-16	PROPER 13
4:25-5:2	PROPER 14
5:15-20	PROPER 15
6:10-20	PROPER 16

PHILIPPIANS
2:5-11	LENT 6 Palm
2:5-11	LENT 6 Passion

1 THESSALONIANS
5:16-24	ADVENT 3

1 TIMOTHY
2:1-7	THANKSGIVING

TITUS
2:11-14	CHRISTMAS EVE/DAY (First)
3:4-7	CHRISTMAS DAY (Second)

HEBREWS
1:1-4, (5-12)	CHRISTMAS (Third)
1:1-4; 2:5-12	PROPER 22
4:12-16	PROPER 23
5:5-10	LENT 5
5:1-10	PROPER 24
7:23-28	PROPER 25
9:11-14	PROPER 26
9:24-28	PROPER 27
10:11-14, (15-18)	PROPER 28

JAMES
1:17-27	PROPER 17
2:1-10, (11-13), 14-17	PROPER 18
3:1-12	PROPER 19
3:13-4:3, 7-8a	PROPER 20
5:13-20	PROPER 21

1 PETER
3:18-22	LENT 1

2 PETER
3:8-15a	ADVENT 2

1 JOHN
1:1-2:2	EASTER 2
3:1-7	EASTER 3
3:16-24	EASTER 4
4:7-21	EASTER 5
5:1-6	EASTER 6
5:9-13	EASTER 7

REVELATION
1:4b-8	CHRIST THE KING
21:1-6a	ALL SAINTS'
21:1-6a	NEW YEARS EVE/DAY

A NOTE CONCERNING LECTIONARIES AND CALENDARS

The following index will aid the user of this book in matching the correct Sunday with the appropriate text during Pentecost. During the Pentecost season, this book lists Sundays by Proper (following the Revised Common and Episcopal lectionary system). Lutheran and Roman Catholic designations indicate days comparable to Sundays on which the Propers are used.

(Fixed dates do not pertain to Lutheran Lectionary)

Fixed Date Lectionaries *Common and Roman Catholic*	Lutheran Lectionary *Lutheran*
The Day Of Pentecost	The Day Of Pentecost
The Holy Trinity	The Holy Trinity
May 29-June 4 — Proper 4, Ordinary Time 9	Pentecost 2
June 5-11 — Proper 5, Ordinary Time 10	Pentecost 3
June 12-18 — Proper 6, Ordinary Time 11	Pentecost 4
June 19-25 — Proper 7, Ordinary Time 12	Pentecost 5
June 26-July 2 — Proper 8, Ordinary Time 13	Pentecost 6
July 3-9 — Proper 9, Ordinary Time 14	Pentecost 7
July 10-16 — Proper 10, Ordinary Time 15	Pentecost 8
July 17-23 — Proper 11, Ordinary Time 16	Pentecost 9
July 24-30 — Proper 12, Ordinary Time 17	Pentecost 10
July 31-Aug. 6 — Proper 13, Ordinary Time 18	Pentecost 11
Aug. 7-13 — Proper 14, Ordinary Time 19	Pentecost 12
Aug. 14-20 — Proper 15, Ordinary Time 20	Pentecost 13
Aug. 21-27 — Proper 16, Ordinary Time 21	Pentecost 14
Aug. 28-Sept. 3 — Proper 17, Ordinary Time 22	Pentecost 15
Sept. 4-10 — Proper 18, Ordinary Time 23	Pentecost 16
Sept. 11-17 — Proper 19, Ordinary Time 24	Pentecost 17
Sept. 18-24 — Proper 20, Ordinary Time 25	Pentecost 18
Sept. 25-Oct. 1 — Proper 21, Ordinary Time 26	Pentecost 19

Oct. 2-8 — Proper 22, Ordinary Time 27	Pentecost 20
Oct. 9-15 — Proper 23, Ordinary Time 28	Pentecost 21
Oct. 16-22 — Proper 24, Ordinary Time 29	Pentecost 22
Oct. 23-29 — Proper 25, Ordinary Time 30	Pentecost 23
Oct. 30-Nov. 5 — Proper 26, Ordinary Time 31	Pentecost 24
Nov. 6-12 — Proper 27, Ordinary Time 32	Pentecost 25
Nov. 13-19 — Proper 28, Ordinary Time 33	Pentecost 26
	Pentecost 27
Nov. 20-26 — Christ The King	Christ The King

Reformation Day (or last Sunday in October) is October 31 (Common, Lutheran)

All Saints' Day (or first Sunday in November) is November 1 (Common, Lutheran, Roman Catholic)